It's a Happy Life

Keys to Successful Enjoyable Living

It's a
Happy Life

Keys to Successful Enjoyable Living

Dr. IAN HERINGA

All rights reserved.

ISBN: 098496973X

ISBN-13: 978-0-9849697-3-9 (Living Publications)

Copyright © 2011 Dr. IAN HERINGA

All rights reserved. Except as permitted under the U.S. Copyright Act of 1976, no part of this publication may be reproduced, distributed, or transmitted in any form or by any means, or stored in a database or retrieval system, without the prior written permission of the publisher.

Scripture quotations noted AMP are from *The Amplified Bible*.. Copyright © 1954, 1958, 1962, 1965, 1987 by the Lockman Foundation. All rights reserved. (www.Lockman.org)

Scripture quotations noted NIV are from The Holy Bible, New International Version® NIV®. Copyright © 1973, 1978, 1984, 2011 by Biblica, Inc. ™ All rights reserved worldwide.

Scripture quotations noted NLT are from the *Holy Bible,* New Living Translation, copyright © 1996, 2004. Tyndale House Publishers, Inc., Wheaton, Illinois 60189. All rights reserved.

Scripture quotations noted The Message are taken from *The Message*. Copyright © 1993, 1994, 1995, 1996, 200, 2001, 2002. NavPress Publishing Group.

Living Publications

www.livingpublications.cc

The publisher is not responsible for websites (or their content) that are not owned by the publisher.

Printed in the United States of America

First Edition: December 2011

All rights reserved.

ISBN: 098496973X

ISBN-13: 978-0-9849697-3-9 (Living Publications)

To Mary Jane, my beautiful wife and closest friend –
You are the fun, and inspiration of my life. After 28 years of being married to you, I am still so inspired by your spirit of excellence. I'm continually challenged, because you have such a kind, sensitive, and giving heart.

To Joy, the most beautiful daughter –
Your love of life, and passion to be in your destiny is so good to see. You have the gift of being liked, and you use it to help people be their best. Your communication skills are ground-breaking. And you are a song in our family.

To my son Josh -
I am excited about your obvious potential for leadership. You have an incredible gift of discerning and understanding people. Your mind is extremely keen. You know how to keep yourself, and your life a happy one. You have shown how you are motivated, and unafraid to take on new challenges.

I love and enjoy all of you so much, and am committed to bringing out the best in you for your future and dreams.

I dedicate this book to Mary Jane, Joy, and Joshua.

CONTENTS

PART I
Looking Out for You

CHAPTER 1   1
    Pursued by Happiness

CHAPTER 2   12
    Your Desires Fulfilled

CHAPTER 3   25
    Promoted by Your Enemies

CHAPTER 4   36
    You Don't Have to be Strong on Your Own

CHAPTER 5   48
    Love Will Heal You

CHAPTER 6   68
    Imagine You: Walking Tall

PART II
Dream Again

CHAPTER 7   83
    Rise Above Your Past

CHAPTER 8   94
    Do Your Little Bit

CHAPTER 9   107
    You Don't Need to Lack

CHAPTER 10   115
    You are Being Carried

CHAPTER 11   125
    Extraordinary Will Come Looking for You

PART III
You are Loved

CHAPTER 12   139
    Your Holiday is Waiting

CHAPTER 13   149
    What Do You Need To Succeed?

CHAPTER 14   160
    I Receive

CHAPTER 15   169
    Appreciate Your Own Talents

CHAPTER 16   179
    The Grass is Greener on Your Side

PART IV
Generous Goodness

CHAPTER 17   189
    Over and Above

CHAPTER 18   199
    God is Proud of You

CHAPTER 19   206
    Exceptional Health

PART V
Fulfilling Your Destiny

CHAPTER 20   213
    Enriching Lives

CHAPTER 21   226
    You're Almost There

CHAPTER 22   237
    You're Well Able

CHAPTER 23   246
    Celebrating Life

Part I

Looking Out for You

CHAPTER 1

PURSUED BY HAPPINESS

Sitting in a Turkish jail, the air was filled with terror. The cement floor and the steel iron bars solidified the fact that Joe and I weren't going anywhere.

I wondered if we were going to be tortured.

I wondered when I would see my wife Mary Jane again.

I wondered when I would play with my children again. My worst nightmare had just come true.

I had not been allowed to make a phone call to contact anyone. As a Canadian citizen, I wanted to call my embassy. But now, no one knew where we were. No one knew where to find us. The fear began to creep in. But no!

Another prisoner, a boy about 15 years old, kept crying and pleading to be let out to go to the bathroom. Finally, the jailer released him from his cell. He gave him a swift kick that sent him flying towards the bathroom. Joe and I were shocked.

Would we be next? My heart went out to the boy.

I wondered, *How come he's being held here at such a young age?*

Hour after hour, sitting there on the bench together with Joe, I felt my hope of release dwindling away.

CAKE IN JAIL

I heard a commotion. Someone was coming! The door swung open.

"You have a visitor," the guard said, stroking his beard.

Much to my surprise, it was the same police detective named Ahmet Bey. Ahmet Bey had previously arrested Joe and I at the bus station.

"Here! Eat." The police detective opened up a package.

"It's from home. My wife baked it."

He unwrapped the package and gave me a fork. My mouth began to water. I looked at the package suspiciously. But we were starving, and hadn't eaten in a while.

Eating cake in jail! Of all things, I thought. Joe and I dug into that cake ravenously. It was good!

From that point on, my hope began to return. I began to dream of getting out again. I began to imagine being reunited with my family. I began to envision being out in the sun again. My despair began to lift, and my hope began to grow.

Along the journey of life, God knows you really need acts of kindness to keep you going and motivated.

"How kind the Lord is! How good he is! So merciful, this God of ours!" Psalm 116:5 (NLT).

God used an act of kindness to remind us that we weren't forgotten.

Even seemingly small acts of kindness can give you strength to face your day.

You might have had some bad breaks, but now it's time for you to have a treat.

Here, eat some cake!

GUARANTEED SUCCESS

First of all as you read this book, I want you to know that you can live a happy life.

You are a person full of incredible potential. You are somebody who is full of dreams and destiny.

"Yes, happy (blessed, fortunate, prosperous, to be envied) are the people whose God is the Lord!" (Psalm 144:15 AMP).

That means you!

Don't think you can just trudge through life, living each day without a lot of good cheer. God wants your heart to be filled with purpose, so that the joy of living is restored and added. This amazing life that God has for us is a full life.

You might wonder how you're going to get there. You might not have the strength to go on. You might dread waking up in the morning, or struggle with going out and leaving the house to go to work.

Well, I've been there too. And now I'm going to help you.

Just think of this book as your piece of cake – a treat that will put a smile on your face, and help you dream again.

You are in need of a major download of encouragement. And you need it now! You don't have to tough it out all the time.

Jesus said, "How often I have wanted to gather your children together as a hen protects her chicks beneath her wings, but you wouldn't let me." (Luke 13:34 NLT).

Jesus uses a very compassionate illustration to show His heart for you.

He is compassionate towards you today. God wants to surround you with His love, as the mother hen protects her chicks. It's time for you to be surrounded in love.

You need to be reminded of who you are. Nothing is impossible for you. Because many times, we forget way too easy.

This is a time to sit back, relax, and receive. I want to remind you of your future, your destiny, and why you have a special place in the world.

You have a special work to do that will make the world a better place. I'm here to stir up what you already know is true about yourself. God is for you and has excellent plans for you (Jeremiah 29:11). You were created with unique inborn talents to help you through life.

Whatever you're feeling like right now, don't quit. The doors of your future are wide open! Just a little bit more, and you will be there. Keep one foot in front of the other foot, and you'll stay on course.

You will be arriving soon. The pain and confusion, rejection, helplessness can't hold you back - because you want God's heart. God hears those cries in the middle of the night. God's heart is for you.

His love for you is what sets you apart. You are a person of dynamic potential. And now is the time for you!

Just because some of the air has run out of your tires doesn't mean it's over for you.

You were created with purpose. You were created with a dream. And you can make your impact on our world.

You can have a happy life!

You are not the exception!

YOU ARE READY, SURPRISE!

Let's go back to the Turkish jail. A week beforehand, a large book order of Turkish New Testaments had come into my office. So I left with my friend Joe to go into Eastern Turkey to deliver the books.

We jumped off the bus, leaving our big boxes in the baggage claim at the bus station. Taking some of our stock with us, we walked through the cobblestone streets of this strange and exotic city.

We eventually found the first store and delivered their order. A "customer" bought one of our books, and started to read it right in the store. I was excited! He eagerly browsed through the New

Testament.

Then, the storeowner sent us to the next store down the street.

In the second store we found three people behind a desk. They sat there, cold and uninviting. They stared at me, unblinking.

One of them, the storeowner, said he had three other bookstores and would like to put in a large order.

I thought, "Oh! A big customer! Great!"

After leaving some samples, we left and explored the rest of the city. It was a beautiful city - half rural, half urban type. And the Turkish food at the café on the corner was delicious!

After we had grabbed lunch, we headed to the bus station to catch our bus, ready to go home!

Then something quite strange happened. The "store owner" from the second store arrived at the bus station while we were waiting for our bus.

Then, came an even bigger surprise! He opened up his wallet, flashed an ID, exactly the same way it's done on television.

"I'm police. Come with me," he commanded sternly.

GOD'S IN A GOOD MOOD ABOUT YOU

God created you. When God made you, He said, "This is good!" There are no regrets on His part. You are His success story.

The Bible says that God sings over you.

"He will take delight in you with gladness. With his love, he will calm all your fears. He will rejoice over you with joyful songs." (Zeph. 3:17 NLT).

Let me put it this way, it is a big deal when important people say good things about you. Now realize this. God our Creator has written songs about you.

This means that if God had a radio station, your song would come on often. God is so happy about you, that He writes songs about you.

His song about you is always on the top ten lists!

God is pleased with you and no one can take that away. He has good thoughts about you.

Psalm 139:17 says, "How precious are your thoughts about me, O

God. They cannot be numbered!" (NLT)

God is in a good mood about you today. God enjoys you today! And He's still singing His song about you.

DON'T WORRY, BE HAPPY

Upon our arrival, the police station was full of activity. My friend Joe and I were petrified. We seemed to be the action here in town. I desperately tried to decipher all the Turkish sentences the police were shouting out in the other room, but it was no use. I strained my ear to listen.

Different police detectives were sent in to interrogate us. First, a nice friendly type was sent in. He would question us. Then, a rough, burly type detective would interrogate us. Then, the nice guy would come in. Then, another rough, burly detective would shout at us. It seemed to be the strategy. We weren't given an opportunity to phone anyone, not even a lawyer.

We had nothing to tell them. We were not spies. We were not foreign agents. I had moved from Canada to Turkey with my family. We help the poor and refugees with clothing and food. I had a book company that distributed various books, and the highest in demand was always the New Testament. The detectives seemed to think that we were part of some plot and conspiracy to overthrow the country.

Joe and I were locked up. As time passed, we took turns sleeping on the bench and on the floor.

I couldn't sleep much, so I paced back and forth, back and forth in the cell until my legs ached.

I wrestled with my thoughts, *Why is this happening to me? What will happen to me? It's already been three days. Now I'm stuck in a Turkish jail. And worse yet, I might never get out!*

UNENDING LOVE FOR YOU

My thoughts were still running wild, so I decided it was time to help myself be happy. I knew from past experience that in times like this, I needed to look to God.

Psalm 100:4-5 says, "Give thanks to him and praise his name. For the LORD is good. His unfailing love continues forever, and his faithfulness continues to each generation." (NLT)

It was time to start thanking the Lord for whatever I could think of. The fear in the jail was overwhelming.

I grabbed my music player and put on my headphones. With my head bobbing to the music and my hands up in the air, I began to worship Jesus. I knew He's protecting me at this time.

But while I was singing, I didn't realize that the guard had come and was staring straight at me.

"Hey! You! What are you doing?" the guard said menacingly.

"I am singing and praying," I replied.

At that point, the guard asked if I could translate the lyrics for him. I am sure he had never seen a prisoner sing in his jail before!

I gave the guard one earphone and with the other earphone in my ear, we both listened to the music.

I told the guard that Jesus died for his sins and that he could have a brand new life. I shared how receiving forgiveness and following Jesus had brought me purpose and great happiness.

BE GOOD TO YOURSELF

There are many ways that you can enjoy your life. You have a music player within your heart. It's time to encourage yourself.

You are actually a fun-filled person. You can develop a tremendous eye for humor. You are an enjoyable person to have around. See yourself as thoughtful, likable, lovable, and an all-around valuable person.

When you see a storm coming, if you can avoid the storm, do so. If not, find a way to weather it out. Treat yourself to a favorite meal. Watch an inspirational movie. Laugh at a comedy. Eat chocolate. Go to the gym. Help yourself to stay in the place of happiness. God's joy is your strength. (Nehemiah 8:10)

IT'S BETTER THAN IT LOOKS

In the Turkish jail, the horrendous monotony was broken up when we had to go in a room and count our belongings. We had to identify our watches, wallets, keys, etc. The guards had already taken everything from our pockets.

They had collected all of our book samples from the bus station. The guards began to count them. And just as they were counting, another detective stepped in to see what was the big commotion.

I said, "Oh! We're counting New Testaments - God's book of love. Would you like one?"

The detectives would each take a book, and they would have to change the number of books on the official report.

Then another detective would come in again, and ask what was going on.

And again I would say, "Oh! We're counting books - God's book of love. Would you like one?"

So that way, we were able to give out quite a few Turkish New Testaments there - including the other books that we had sold to Ahmet Bey pretending to be a storeowner. Wow! These police were our best customers!

Then it seemed like they were giving us a tour through the facility. It was time to get our mug shots. Flash! Flash!

"Turn your head to the front, and side."

Next came the fingerprinting and ink all over our fingers.

At that point I thought, *This is really serious.*

They took our mug shots and fingerprints and put them on file. Then we were taken back to the jail cell, and locked in. Terror filled the air.

I thought, *This part of the tour I do not like. I want to go home! Help!*

CARRYING YOU

As I expressed before, in every one of life's situations - you need support. You need motivation. You need encouragement.

I will carry you from here - right through to the end of this book.

Because now is your time to break out! Now is your time to be built up. It's time to regroup, and it's time to receive a new strategy for life.

I don't know what's going on in your life as you read. You might have picked up this book, feeling bad about yourself. Maybe you feel that you messed up on that last job interview. Or perhaps you are about to be laid off.

Romans 8:1 says, "So now there is no condemnation for those who belong to Christ Jesus." (NLT).

This means that there is a sign saying *"No Condemnation"*.

Maybe you are in debt, paying daily interest on your credit cards. The worry and fear is gnawing you and weighing you down.

Perhaps you picked up this book feeling like you don't belong anywhere. Maybe you feel that you don't have any real friends or anyone you can trust. Again, the sign says, *"No Condemnation."*

Maybe you picked up this book because someone whom you trusted has just betrayed you. That someone should've known better. And that someone should've loved you for who you really are.

But I think the real reason that you picked up this book is that you have a deep hunger to be filled up.

You have a dream, and you want to do well.

Your dream needs to happen. There is help for you.

PULLING FOR YOU

You definitely need somebody pulling for you. I have seen time and time again that God cares for His children extraordinarily.

You are someone that God likes. He has plans for you, to give you a hope and a future. He wants to deposit good things into your life. He will not leave you alone. He will not leave you where you are. So don't feel abandoned just yet.

Isaiah 40:31 says, "But those who trust in the LORD will find new strength. They will soar high on wings like eagles. They will run and not grow weary. They will walk and not faint." (NLT)

As you pray, cry out, and trust in God - you will find that your burdens get lighter because He is carrying you. You will begin to see His supernatural solutions come into place. And you will realize that what you can't do - God will do! And more!

God will mark your life with acts of kindness that will also lighten your load. Get ready because your journey with Him is as exciting as ever!

Believe it or not, you have the inner strength. You must realize that you have what it takes! You are empowered for this time. You are stronger than you think, and you have the power to succeed. God cares for you and carries you, so much so that you will feel like you are soaring!

This is true happiness.

CHAPTER 2

YOUR DESIRES FULFILLED

In my wallet, I always carry around the copy of a page of the Turkish Constitution, right there with my driver's license. After being arrested and harassed by the police and military over 50 times, I never leave home without it.

Whenever I'd get arrested again, I'd whip out my wallet, show my page of the Turkish Constitution, and petition my rights.

"According to your Constitution, I am guaranteed freedom of religion."

The page of the Turkish Constitution, guaranteeing freedom of religion had been folded and refolded.

"You are unlawfully arresting me and I should be released."

I'd also show them a copy of a court decision. That piece of paper declared that I was free to distribute New Testaments and that the New Testament was not an illegal book – contrary to popular opinion.

But then there were times that the policemen said, "I don't care. I am the law. And you will go to jail if I wish."

At that, I was dumbfounded. I was so shocked, I couldn't think of anything to say.

THE BOOK THAT LOVES

The following conversation is still etched in my memory. It was a beautiful summer day. The sun was shining, and the seagulls were flying overhead. A warm breeze was bringing in the scent of the Marmara Sea.

Sitting across from me on the porch was a Kurdish freedom fighter. Ali had just gotten out of jail.

"I had to say thanks, Ian. I have decided to stop being a terrorist. I met one of your staff the other day. He gave me a Turkish New Testament," Ali said, waving his New Testament out of his pocket and waving it in the air. "I made my decision to leave terrorism because I believe the message of the book of love."

I wish everyone could have the opportunity to read this book. I wish it was available and on the market," Ali continued.

Ali's words stayed with me. Living in Turkey was beautiful, but I wanted to do something bigger.

Religious freedom is important. I had the freedom in Canada to research all the religions. And when people tell me they've always wanted to read the New Testament – I'm going to give them that opportunity. Through reading the New Testament, my own life was changed.

The more I tried to forget Ali and his plea, the more his words wouldn't leave me. I began to dream.

And I knew I had to be willing to risk! Everyone said it was impossible. All my friends said it wouldn't work. They told me I would get arrested.

And so I started the first book company. I named it Meshur

(famous). My dream was to make the New Testament famous in Turkey.

Now, the Turkish Religious Affairs Department calls New Testament distribution as one of the foremost strategies, and as one of the well-known Christian services in Turkey.

What's your dream? God will do it!

WEAKNESS QUALIFIES YOU

But in the beginning, I first had to learn Turkish.

A tall Turkish man breathed down my neck, and demanded to know why I was in the Turkish teahouse.

"Who are you? Where did you come from? Why are you here?" His questions came at me, fast and furious.

Sticking his long wiry finger in my face, he accused me of being some type of agent with the CIA, Mossad, or Interpol. I guess he had noticed my sunglasses. All the men in the teashop stopped talking and turned to watch. The air itself turned hostile.

I thought, "I need to get out of here!" I began to feel nauseous, and looked for a quick exit.

Everyday, I would pick a route through the city, visiting the various Turkish businesses in order to practice my Turkish.

Next on my route was another teahouse. I sat down at a table and ordered some tea. Soon, another man cornered me. He too demanded to know what I was doing in the Turkish teahouse. Panic rose in my heart. I was sure everyone in the teahouse could hear my heart thumping loudly in my chest.

I thought, *Help! I need to get out of here now!* As soon as he looked the other direction, I slipped out.

I went home to my sweet wife Mary Jane and told her what had happened.

"You know, I really can't learn this language anymore. I'm too crippled. My spirit is broken with fear," I said.

I didn't have the courage anymore. I wanted to give up. I really didn't have the "get up and go" anymore. I'd have stomach cramps, and I could be found curled up on my bed at times. The pain was unbearable. Spasm after spasm would wash over me, and I'd end up running to the bathroom to vomit. But worse, the pain in my heart began to kill my spirit.

You don't have what it takes. You are failing. And you won't be able to fulfill your dreams. You are so weak. You can't even leave the house without fear.

The condemning thoughts played in my mind, again and again. Not knowing what else to do, I wanted to quit.

YOU ARE SUPPORTED

It was Sunday morning, and I was headed for church in Berlin. It was a small congregation of expatriates and their families. At the end of the service, Pastor James asked if there was anybody who needed to be prayed for.

I went forward. I was desperate. My dream was hanging by a thread. And I was too crippled by fear to move on.

I quietly told him, "Pastor James, I'm struggling with fear! I can't fulfill my dream in Turkey."

As soon as he heard the secret I had just whispered to him, Pastor James turned around, and told the whole church!

The whole congregation just stared at me with pity.

The poor guy. He'll never make a good preacher. I'm sure that is what the old ladies on the front row were thinking.

I felt so embarrassed. I wished I could disappear through the floor. I almost hid behind the pulpit. This was worse than my nightmares. Now everybody knew my struggle!

Pastor James and the church prayed for me, "God, you won't give up on Ian. And we won't give up on him either."

Soon, I was back at it again, visiting different Turkish teahouses. A courage miracle had taken place in my life.

YOUR GIANTS ARE BIG ENOUGH TO FALL

Feeling too small for the job is not an uncommon feeling. The problem is when that feeling begins to control you. The reality is you are big enough for the job! You have what it takes! You are the one with the dream. You own it. And you will walk through open door after open door. Nothing can stop you.

In the Bible, 12 spies were sent out to scout out the Promised Land. Of those twelve spies, ten of them came back with a discouraging report to tell the people of Israel.

They told everyone, "The land is beautiful! It is a rich and prosperous country. But there are giants in the land. The giants are too big for us. We cannot win."

And by believing this negative report, their generation did not enter the Promised Land because of the giants. They did not receive what God had planned for them.

On the other hand, there once was a shepherd boy named David. A giant named Goliath was oppressing Israel. David wanted to enlist in the army, but he was too young.

One day, David saw Goliath the giant. He said to himself, *Yes, he's big... big enough to fall down!* David took a sling and 5 round stones. He hit the giant in the head with the first stone. And BAM! The giant came tumbling down.

Every giant that stands before you is the same. When you see a problem, just remember that giants are big enough to fall down. And you are big enough to step over every fallen giant.

Just think back about how you have stepped over giants before. You've faced a new job, you've paid off a debt, you've stepped out to try, and overcome an addiction.

"For by You I can run through a troop. And by my God I can leap over a wall." (Psalm 18:29 AMP)

EVERYDAY - A BRAND NEW YOU

That is what makes up your history. Now is the time to step over a few more giants. And make some more history!

Your history gathered up, makes for a brand new you!

Have you ever been in a situation where you had a dream, but not the strength to carry it out? I never did well in elementary and high school. My grades were just barely good enough for me to pass.

And when I arrived in Turkey, I struggled for some years to learn

Turkish. To do anything in Turkey – you needed to know the Turkish language. This was an undeniable fact.

Words like "muvaffakiyetsizlestiricilestiriveremeyebileceklerimizdenmissinizcesine" baffled me. Turkish carries the potential for infinite word length. I came to terms with the fact that I just couldn't get my tongue around the language. And yet in my head, an impossible plan began to hatch.

You see this was my plan. Some Turks that I had encountered complained of the fact that they had never had the chance to even touch a Turkish New Testament. Distributing the book would be dangerous. It would be risky. But you know what? It would be an adventure!

"Ian, you are crazy. You'll get yourself killed," some said with an incredulous look on their face when I told them.

Others said, "Ha! You won't be able to last one week."

Even my closest friends said tactfully, "Ian, are you sure about this? This is the wildest strategy I've ever heard. And if I see you on the street getting arrested – I'm going to walk the other direction."

But some of the people I looked up to told me, "Ian, go for it!"

I decided to put my dream in action. My knees were literally shaking as I put on my coat and left the house. I met friend after friend at designated teashops. I'd greet them with the customary Turkish greeting, shake their hand, and at the same time, slip a New Testament into their pocket. They'd whisper thanks, and make for the nearest exit.

That day, I gave out about 20 copies of the New Testament to my Turkish friends.

THERE IS HOPE FOR YOU

I got home, and collapsed on the couch. At that point, I was too afraid of being arrested or deported out of the country. I was too fearful to do anything more.

Again, I was powerless. I'd pace back and forth in my apartment, my fears winning one minute, and my dream winning the next. I had a half-day of prayer during which I plunked myself down on the carpet. I promised God I wouldn't get up until I had an answer. On my face on the floor, soaking the carpet with my tears, I felt so weak.

I cried out to God, "God, you know my dream. The New Testament was the book that carried me out of drugs to living a changed life. I know it's Your book of love. So many people have told me they'd like to read the New Testament. But it's not readily available. I'm the man with a dream. But now, I don't know if I even have the strength to do this."

YOU WILL CONQUER THOSE FEARS

The following morning, I got out of bed with purpose in my heart. I got dressed to go out to the barbershop. On my way out the door, I looked in the mirror and saw a six-foot Canadian, wearing a Columbia ski jacket and jeans, and sneakers.

Two weeks later, after the visit to the barber and a trip to the local market, I hardly recognized myself. I had grown a big Turkish moustache. Sporting sunglasses, and a brown leather jacket, even my wife Mary Jane was shocked at the new look. Dressy pants and shoes completed the new image. I picked up my new black briefcase, and from that day forward – I was never seen without it.

When my little daughter Joy saw me, she laughed. "Daddy, you look like an 007 Agent!"

Driven by a powerful God-given urge to accomplish the impossible, I found some secondhand booksellers that wanted to be my distributors for the Turkish New Testament. That day, I was able to get out 66 copies of the New Testament - God's message of love. One of the guys even asked me where I had gotten my new sunglasses!

The following week I thought, *All this half-day praying stuff really works*!

I was so amazed at how God had answered my prayer! I had another half day of prayer. I prayed, "God, I am really enjoying this escapade. But now give me strength, because I'm about to walk out the door. I feel so weak."

That day, I saw 120 Turkish New Testaments go out!

The dream that lies dormant in your heart will sometimes only be awakened by a cry of desperation. Facing your situation head on, realizing your weakness – that is sometimes the hardest thing to do.

YOUR VERY STRUGGLE IS YOUR STRENGTH

But God knows the dream is in your heart. He is the one that puts it there. He is sympathetic with your weakness and will step in to see you overcome! God will hear that cry of desperation, the cry of loneliness. Guaranteed, help will come.

2 Corinthians 12:9 says, "My grace is sufficient for you, for my power is made perfect in weakness."

When you have run out of your own strength and you know it, the Lord touches your heart with His supernatural strength.

Success breeds confidence. You need to succeed. It is an innate desire that you can't get rid of.

YOU WERE BORN TO WIN

I began seeing hundreds of New Testaments go out every week. Bookstores wanted them, libraries sent in requests. Jails and universities excitedly awaited their copies of the New Testament. We even went door to door, and heard a lot of housewives squeal with delight.

And if I didn't come home for supper, my wife and kids would know I had been arrested.

Sometimes the police would arrest me, other times it was the military.

"Daddy, Daddy! What happened? Do you have another adventure to tell us? Is that why you are late for supper?" Joy and Josh would ask.

Week after week, we'd head to my depot and load boxes of New Testaments at midnight in order to avert any trouble. In the morning, our team would bring a trolley of New Testaments to various distribution outlets.

Personal requests were shipped out by cargo, arriving at your door, wrapped in brown paper.

YOU HAVE A WAY OUT

Walking down the exotic pedestrian street in Istanbul, the sights and sounds of this ancient city were breathtaking.

Crowds of people hustled past the stores in the historic buildings that line the street.

That day, I had three other men join me as we brought New Testaments to some of the bookstores. A tall South African, a French Canadian, and a Malaysian.

As we were walking, a young man by the name of Recep approached us. A charming young fellow, he spoke fluent English. Recep invited us to come to his uncle's teahouse to sit down and drink tea.

We followed Recep up a side street and down some steps into a Turkish teahouse.

Soon, we were seated in the teahouse drinking the famed Turkish tea.

As we talked with Recep, the whole teahouse crowd gathered around us.

I began to tell them my story. They listened attentively. I told how I had left Canada to live in Turkey. We talked on a wide range of subjects.

Recep and his friends asked questions about Canada. They were curious as to what life was like for us as expatriates living in Turkey. After we finished our tea, the four of us got up to go.

"Well, it was nice meeting you all. Thanks for inviting us for tea." I said politely.

"Hey! Wait a minute! We have something for you," Recep's uncle shouted from across the room.

He handed me a plate with a bill of $175. – just for four little cups of tea.

I thought, *I can't believe it!*
We've walked into a trap!

YOU CAN'T BE OUTNUMBERED

As I stood up to go, two bouncers grabbed me from behind, and pushed me back down in my seat. They stuck their hands in my pocket and grabbed my wallet and my passport.

At that point, I knew we were not going to get out of this. We were outnumbered. Around twenty people surrounded my friends and I. I saw my life flash in front of my eyes.

I've heard about rackets like this. What if they break my arm? What if they beat us up until we're unconscious? How will I get back home to my family? Wild thoughts ran through my head at breakneck speed.

"Isa!" I cried out as loud as I could ("Isa" is the Turkish for Jesus).

The two bouncers grabbed my jaw and tried to force it shut. They turned up the music in the teahouse.

I tried to get free, and cried out, "Isa!" Recep's uncle turned up the music some more.

I cried out "ISA!" a third time at that point.

My Malaysian friend is normally quiet and calm. But he jumped up, stuck his finger in the bouncers' faces and commanded the guys who were holding me down saying,

"I rebuke you in the Name of Jesus. I rebuke you in the Name of Jesus," he shouted with a voice full of authority.

"I rebuke you in the name of Jesus!" Three times. Just like that.

At that point, Recep's uncle gave me back my wallet. The thugs gave me back my passport.

"Okay, you are free to leave," motioned the uncle.

We left that Turkish teahouse amazed.

DON'T HAVE TO BE STRONG ON YOUR OWN

God protects the helpless. He sticks up for the underdog. He puts up a protective security system right around you. When you know you can't get up, and when you're absolutely powerless, don't worry. Don't give up hope just yet. The movie ain't over until the underdog wins!

God has an answer for you. Jesus said, "I have come that they may have life and have it abundantly."

Abundant life means peace, the fulfillment of your dreams. It means that you don't lack anything, whether it is the discipline that gives success, or the strength to overcome an addiction.

When you feel weak, abandoned, and lost, don't give up. No matter what harshness or cruelty you've gone through – you are born to be a winner.

And when you can't do it, God steps in. He'll give you the incredible courage and boldness to face your fears. Psalm 46:1 "God is our refuge and strength, a very present help in trouble." (KJV) He is the producer for your dream and will set you up to win!

God's rules and laws are set. "I will protect you. I will stand up for you. That is who I am. That is my personality. That is what I do."

I have seen how God stepped in and turned everything around. And God wants to do the same for you today! You can go from having no hope – to bringing hope to others. He is a good God. He's good all the time. He's good to everyone who asks. And He has goodness for you.

You don't have to be strong on your own. You don't have to do everything on your own.

You are a perfect candidate to be helped. Loneliness is a thing of the past. Because Someone is on your side, pulling strings for you, making sure that you win.

The Lord has his plans to defend you and to stand up for you. He will lift you up and carry you in His arms.

PLEASED WITH YOU

Keep running. Keep going. Keep smiling and hoping for the best, and you will soon see the results. You're going to see the reward.

To know is to believe. You don't have to wait till you enter the gates of heaven to hear the words,

"Well done, good and faithful servant! You have been faithful with a few things; I will put you in charge of many things. Come and share your master's happiness." (Matthew 25:23 NIV)

You need to see and hear God's encouraging messages right now, and all along the way. God knows you need it!

It says in Psalms 84:11 that, "The Lord will withhold no good thing from those who do what is right." (NLT)

It is a good thing for you to be built up, motivated, and full of passion and vision. So live with abandon. Have some fun. Risk, even if you make mistakes. You are being carried through life.

God rewards you when you try your best, even if you think your best isn't very good.

A reward doesn't mean the normal hourly pay. Reward means bonus!

So keep your eyes on him. You're due for a bonus!

CHAPTER 3

PROMOTED BY YOUR ENEMIES

What a way to spend Christmas, providing thousands of copies of God's message of love - the New Testament to anyone who wanted one!

My team and I were on Istanbul's busiest shopping street giving out gifts – New Testaments for Christmas. Running a promotion for one week only, we sent the word out, and people were coming from all over the city to get their Christmas present from us!

"Okay guys. This is going to be good. If you get attacked – smile. If the reporters come – smile. And when people ask for a New Testament – make sure you really smile."

There were 20 of us. We had set up a table in this central part of town. I got the necessary permissions from the Governor of Istanbul. You see, the Governor's office never thought to check with the police to check my record.

And so I got two fancy pieces of paper with stamps galore — saying that my team could distribute New Testaments for a week.

Everyone was running around, trying to keep up with the stock of Turkish New Testaments on the table. The stream of people coming and getting a Turkish New Testament wouldn't stop! Keeping track, sometimes over 3000 New Testaments would go out in just a few hours.

The whole team was intent on reaching out to people, loving people, giving out the New Testaments to those that had wanted one.

WE LOVE YOU

All of a sudden, a young man showed up with two friends. They started shouting! The three men raised the Turkish flag and began to chant nationalistic slogans.

"Turkey is ours. Ours is Turkey. Turkey is ours. Ours is Turkey."

One man, the head of the local mosque planted himself right in front of me.

"Do you have permission to give out New Testaments?" He shoved me and angrily demanded that we show him our official papers.

A mob began to form. The very air was explosive. All around my team and me, violence was ready to erupt.

Then two TV cameras showed up. The young man who was the leader of the group kicked over our table of New Testaments. He sent everything flying. The mob continued to chant nationalistic slogans.

The team hurried to pick up the New Testaments on the ground. Some of our girls had tears in their eyes. You could see the terror in their faces.

It seemed at any moment, my team and I were all about to be torn to shreds. I was being pushed and shoved around. Everyone around us was shouting and yelling. The TV news cameras were filming everything.

I knew that risk is always rewarded when love is the motive.

'Oh God! Show me what to do!" I whispered.

With God's compassion in my heart, in the face of all the hostility—I raised my voice over all the commotion.

I shouted out real loud, "We love you. The New Testament that we are distributing is God's message of love to you."

That was about all I could say. They began pushing me around even more.

Was this going to be the end?

We heard a siren in the distance as a police car made its way towards us. The police quickly escorted the team and me to safety.

The police dispersed the mob. That evening, the attack was on the TV news all over Turkey.

BE NICE TO EVERYONE, BUT...

Two years later, on the exact same spot, our team was doing our usual Christmas promotional event and providing Turkish New Testaments to those who wanted one.

All of a sudden three guys ran up and grabbed Michael (one of the guys on the team). They began to hit him, and they dragged him over to me.

The attackers demanded to know if we had official permission to give out New Testaments.

Upon learning that we had official permission from the Governor of Istanbul, the ringleader of the group blew up! He was furious! They started to kick and punch Michael.

Soon Michael was on the ground, and the ringleader came after me.

Panic rose in my heart. Instinctively to protect myself, I moved out into the open. The ringleader came at me swinging. As soon as his fist made contact with my jaw, a rapid stream of blood poured out onto the street.

I cried out to God!

My jaw was searing with pain. I could see the guy's fists coming towards me in slow motion.

I thought, *Man! What should I do? I'm a pastor. And pastors are supposed to be nice to everyone. But there is no way that I'm going to get beat up voluntarily.*

YOU HAVE HELP

"God, HELP me!" Everything was a blur.

All of a sudden, it's like I saw something come between the assailant and me. He kept punching. But none of the punches made impact with my body. Every punch landed short. Some barrier was keeping him from hitting me!

Mary Jane also saw some barrier come between the attacker and me, almost like an invisible person. The team saw the phenomenon too. The assailant couldn't make contact no matter how close he got! Their mouths dropped open. *Who and what was that?*

I was being protected!

MY SON THE HERO

My son Josh ran to the nearby police car and whipped open the car door.

"Help! My Dad is being beaten! Help!"

The police arrived on the scene. The policemen took Michael and me and brought us to the hospital. There, the doctor put stitches in my mouth and closed the gaping wound. They gave me a medical report.

I wondered why the main attacker came to the hospital also. He had not been hurt, however he received a medical report as well.

Michael and I found ourselves again in the police car, lights flashing, as we headed to the police station.

When we arrived at the police station, a group of police and the attackers sat down in a room and drank tea. The main attacker seemed to know everyone in the police station and the police were very friendly with him.

Both Michael and I gave our statements and then hurriedly got out of there.

Meanwhile, my precious wife Mary Jane gathered the team together to pray around my blood on the street. No matter how many times I have had troubles, she never gets used to it. It always pains her heart. And now seeing my blood on the ground, she could hardly bear it.

She prayed with the team, "God, this is my husband's blood here on the street. I can't believe what has just happened. I'm still in shock. We are all hurting. We are all afraid. But I thank you for the invisible barrier between my husband and the attackers. You defended him. Lord we forgive the attackers. We ask you for mercy upon them to melt their hearts."

There were tears in everyone's eyes.

BULLIES NEVER WIN

So what do you do when your motive is good, and yet everything goes wrong? What do you do when you have a dream, and yet there's terrible opposition, fighting and even bloodshed?

How do you handle injustice and oppression? First of all, forgiveness is the path to success. Forgiveness sets you free to move on with your life. Don't keep the memories alive by staying bitter. You have life to enjoy, successes awaiting you.

I forgave my assailants when my blood was all over the ground. God forgives you in the same way. He has no hard feelings against you.

You are an important person. And you have important things to do. Taking vengeance will just distract you from succeeding for yourself. Focusing on those who have wronged you will hinder your own future.

Otherwise, you take on the role of being the avenger and it will eat you alive. Whatever you focus on - you become. And you begin to take on the same character qualities as your assailant.

Forgiveness is so hard and painful. But forgiveness always wins. Forgiving others shows that you've been forgiven a lot. It shows that you are loved.

Your destiny is too important to be wasted on being bitter.

Forgiveness always brings a lightened load.

Many times, I've seen God defending me, God backing me up. When I forgive, I put the situation in God's hands. He takes hold of the situation. I look to Him for justice.

Bullies never win.

PROMOTED BY YOUR ABUSER

"God's Message of Love to you," those words would keep burning in the first attacker's heart.

He couldn't sleep, couldn't forget. Many nights for two years, he mulled on those words.

Soon, an idea began to form in his head. A plot emerged, then a storyline, a movie script – for he was a movie producer. The attacker would stay up, night after night, feverishly working on his new project. And then! It was show time!

A film crew arrived on the scene—the exact spot of the second attack where my blood was on the street and where Mary Jane prayed with our team for their hearts to melt.

The crew set up their cameras and lights to film scenes of a Warner Brothers movie.

Actors poured out of vans, and began to take their places, as they reenacted the main scene of the movie—the attack on our New Testament book table.

This movie [movie name withheld in order to protect those involved] became a widely acclaimed blockbuster Turkish movie released by Warner Brothers. It played in every single theater throughout the country, and you can buy the DVD in the Turkish grocery stores.

The synopsis of the plot goes something like this. "A freshman in university gets more and more involved in extremism. In his search for meaning and reality, he plans to become a suicide bomber.

But then, he comes in contact with the ASLAN International team as they distribute Turkish New Testaments on the streets of Istanbul saying, 'God's message of love to you!' "

The movie is based on a true story—the producer's own story. The words of "God's Message of Love" have prevailed!

WORDS OF COMPASSION PENETRATE HEARTS

We discovered that the actual producer of the movie was the same man that had kicked over our New Testament table and started the mob against us. We were shocked!

Sitting in the movie theater, munching popcorn, I pulled the brim of my cap lower. Hopefully, no one would notice me. I mulled over this turn of events.

I wonder what produced the change of heart in this man's life. He went from attacking us to doing penance by creating a movie about a suicide bomber coming in contact with our team - giving out God's message of love.

My mind wandered some more.

I hope he's okay. I read in the newspaper that the police arrested him. They think I actually financed this movie. But hey! At least they weren't successful in censoring it. The movie's already a big hit in Turkey.

God wanted them to understand that the New Testament is His message of love to them. The Turkish nation is loved.

Many newspapers and websites discussed this whole event in the movie. Columnists and movie critics wrote that God's message of love was so prominent. It was the overriding factor in the movie.

"This movie must have been financed by the Christians who distribute New Testaments," the editors wrote.

The actor of the film said in the ensuing TV interviews, "Well, my favorite part of the movie is the New Testament distribution. In fact, when we were shooting that scene – a nationalistic young guy tried to attack me,"

The actor grinned, "But my producer grabbed the young guy by the scruff of his neck and told him to get out. I guess he didn't realize we were filming a movie."

"But yeah. That part about God's message of Love, it impacted me. It impacted my life."

RADICALLY LOVED

God's love is always radical. Your behavior doesn't affect His opinion of you. God's love always builds up. And today God loves you and has plans for you - to give you hope and a future.

God's love sets you free and gives you confidence. It makes you feel that you can do nothing wrong. It is true. Every mistake you make can be forgiven.

Sometimes you might feel like a little boy who falls down, and then he has to get picked up and dusted off. The falling down is the painful part. But the dusting off and picking up part is what God does for us.

God's always looking out for you, lifting you up, encouraging you, motivating you. He's always protecting you, giving to you, and bringing promotion into your life. God's love is always rearranging situations so that you look good. Love brings success. Will you receive His love?

YOUR ATTACKERS WILL BECOME YOUR FANS

A meeting was arranged with the former attacker who had gone on to produce this Warner Brothers blockbuster movie.

We went with a lot of apprehension and forgiveness. Forgiveness is a lifestyle.

I hope we're doing the right thing here. This guy attacked us once, he might do it again. I thought as I emptied my pockets. If we were ambushed, at least they won't get my wallet! Or my Canadian passport!

"Okay! Let's go!"

My associate and I walked down that same street where we had been mobbed. I walked past the place where Mary Jane and the team had prayed around my blood on the street.

I struggled with my thoughts. *Was I being naïve? Were we walking into a trap? Of course you have to forgive, but sometimes people will just go on to hurt you more.*

But in my heart, I could begin to feel the thaw. There was a love for the attacker and it was from God.

My associate and I were led to a basement store, where we waited for the producer to arrive. That sure was nerve wracking! The guys in the store watched us suspiciously. They wondered why we wanted to meet with their friend.

I looked around the store, keeping an eye out for any hidden guns, sticks, or knives. I wasn't going to take any chances.

I sat on the edge of my seat, ready to run at any given time. My associate watched me intently, watching for the signal in case we should have to make a run for it. So we waited.

Half an hour later, the producer arrived. Sunglasses and long curly hair, he certainly looked the Hollywood type.

He swaggered into the store, stuck his hand out to shake, and then I saw his lip quiver.

LIFE IS STRANGER THAN FICTION

"Oh! I know you! You're the... the... the...," he stuttered.

"Um... I'm sorry," he blurted. "...For everything."

Together, we found a Starbucks nearby and sat down at a table. Although he was trying his best to look cool, I could see his hands shaking.

"Ian, I have something to say."

"Sure," I replied as I sipped my caramel macchiato.

"Pastor. I did you wrong. I attacked you. I kicked over your table. I terrorized your team. I did wrong. And I want you to know that I am sorry. Will you forgive me?"

I looked into his eyes.

"I forgive you," I replied. You could see his obvious relief.

"Pastor. There is no evil in your eyes. I'm really, really sorry to have attacked a man such as yourself."

I smiled back at him.

"And Ian," he grinned, "sometimes life is stranger than fiction! Don't you think this very scene right now would make a great movie? Wanna do a sequel?"

OCEAN OF LOVE

God is a God of love. His love for you is so complete. You can do nothing to exempt yourself from this love.

It is so enormous that it reaches across every culture and every language. His love transcends across borders, it reaches to good and evil. It reaches to the kind and unkind, the merciful and merciless.

Right now you might be thinking that you are being treated wrongly. You are only seeing the opposite of what you deserve or expect. And right now you might not see the answer that you want.

But now is the time to trust. God will come through for you. God always shows up. God is the one who's ever near, and ever present. He's in complete control over every chaos.

God is never unkind in His actions. He reaches down and has compassion on all our problems. Because he is God, He is in control over everything. He has complete oversight over everything because He is the Creator.

And many times, we find it hard to see the big picture.

You might think you're always in a rut. You might think that nothing good ever happens to you. You might label yourself a failure. But just hang on and trust. As you trust God, not one moment of your life will be wasted. You are always His top priority.

That's why we have to trust. But why do we trust? Because God loves you and has a bigger dream for your life than you do. So He cares about every detail and every problem that happens in your life. And don't worry. He'll make sure that despite the abuse, you will win! He is kind to you, gracious to you.

Psalm 23:6 says, "Surely your goodness and love will follow me all the days of my life."

It's time for you to experience God's goodness.

CHAPTER 4

YOU DON'T HAVE TO BE STRONG ON YOUR OWN

It was not an easy time to be a Christian in Turkey. The Turkish police had been arresting Christians all over the country - assuming them to have some foreign motive to take over the country.

Some of my friends had already been arrested, so I decided to go and see Bill and Henry. I needed to find out the latest developments in the wave of arrests. Bill and Henry would know what was happening.

Upon arrival, I knocked on the door of the basement apartment. Nobody answered.

I knocked again. After a few moments, one of my friends unlocked the door. As the door slowly swung open, I saw two plainclothes policemen searching the apartment.

Books from the bookshelves lay all over on the ground. Wide eyed, I didn't waste a moment.

I casually said, "Well, I guess I better go."

Spinning around, I slammed the door shut in their faces, and ran up 2 flights of stairs.

I ran out the front door. A police van was parked, blocking the driveway. Another one of my Christian friends had been picked up and was sitting in the van.

I ran past the van. The two police came running out of the apartment building and started chasing me. They radioed the guys in the van to follow me as well.

My exit to the street was blocked! I had nowhere to go. A green fence stood between freedom and me. I vaulted over it and just kept running. I could hear the police shouting behind the fence.

I was so thankful to God for giving me long legs! In school, I was always the fastest runner. I ran down the road, past my apartment, and past the store where my wife buys bread. I ran across the street and turned left into a side street. Ducking into a small doorway, I tried to catch my breath.

I found myself in a children's bookstore. I headed towards the back of the store, and out of breath, I picked up a children's book and started reading!

The book was upside down. But I didn't care.

I caught my breath. *I think I lost them!*

YOU ARE NEVER ALONE

Here I was alone, pretending to read children's books at a bookstore. My friends were arrested and on their way perhaps to a Turkish jail. I had no idea where they were being taken.

But right now I felt so forlorn. I began to pray for my friends, to pray for my family, to pray for myself. I was overwhelmed and bewildered at that moment.

I was afraid.

But it says, "Taste and see that the Lord is good. Oh, the joys of those who take refuge in him." (Psalm 34:8 NLT)

I went home, and told God, "I want to learn about your goodness. I want to understand your mercy. And I want to experience your compassion."

And now, I have tasted and seen for 25 years in Turkey that God is good. To tell you the truth, my life has been a lot of fun.

When you taste something with your mouth, it registers in your memory. The escapades that I have been through have brought me to believe and hold on to the fact that God is good.

YOU ARE ALREADY IN THE WINNER'S CIRCLE

The Bible says, "When God is for us, who can be against us!" Romans 8:31(NIV)

No one can stop you when you are following the dream God has for your life. God's dream for you is wrapped up in mercy. He is compassionate towards you. He understands. God's love for you is not dependent on your performance.

He cares about your recent divorce. He cares about your children when they are not doing well in school. He cares when you can't make ends meet.

He cares about the foreclosure proceedings. He cares that you feel bored in your job. He cares about you losing weight and feeling good about yourself. God absolutely cares.

Don't worry. It's okay. You don't have to strive and do it all. You don't have to be perfect to make things work out. When you can't help yourself, this is actually a secretly envied place - where nothing you can do is going to help, no matter what.

You need a miracle! You have put yourself in an elitist place – the Miracle Needer's Club. This is actually the winner's circle.

The situation that you are most worried about can turn out to be your biggest miracle. This is the time where you need everything to turn around. Your problem can become your launching pad for success!

Being part of the Miracle Needer's Club is about to propel you into a place of peace and rest that you never thought possible.

The peace that you are about to experience will knock the impossibilities off your shoulders. You don't have to carry the burden alone.

And you are about to enter a place of rest that you haven't experienced for years. You are about to feel more rested than you ever thought possible. Because you are in the Miracle Receiver's Club. Read on and receive.

HARD-HITTING PRAYERS

My family and I were enjoying our hamburgers and fries at the Turkish McDonald's. What a treat! Finally, we could have another taste of home.

As I sipped my milkshake, I noticed a great commotion coming from the other side of the restaurant. People were fighting, swinging chairs, and fist fighting.

I found myself in a McDonald's war zone! Guys all over the restaurant were pushing, shoving, fighting, and screaming. I was with my wife and kids and trying to protect them.

"C'mon honey. We have to get out of here," I told Mary Jane.

Two men that were fighting blocked our exit. We couldn't get past them on the narrow staircase.

So I prayed for the guys to stop fighting. All of a sudden, they instantly stopped fighting in front of us. We were able to pass and get to a safe corner.

The staff barred the doorways as gangs outside tried to break the glass and enter the restaurant. The staff whisked us out a back door, and I was able to get my family out of the restaurant safely.

NO, I DIDN'T HIT YOU

After things settled down, one of the two guys who had been blocking our exit during the fighting saw me.

He angrily accosted me, "Why did you hit me!"

I replied gently, "No I didn't hit you. Why would I hit you anyway? But I did pray for you."

He was shocked. He thought I had really hit him. But whatever happened to him - it made him stop fighting.

Must've been a hard-hitting prayer!

RELEASED FROM YOUR FEARS

The story of David always inspires me. David was a young man who was to become king. His brothers were against him. People were talking about him behind his back and trying to bring him down.

One of his main enemies was King Saul. David said in 2 Samuel 22:44, "You have delivered me from the attacks of the peoples." (NIV)

In every attack — you are eligible for deliverance. David wrote in Psalm 30:27 "You are my hiding place." (NIV)

Whatever fighting is going on around you, God hides you. He hides you from the attacks of jealousy and envy. He hides you from attacks on your finances.

He hides you from attacks on your name and reputation. He hides you from the intrigues of others who are intent on making you look bad.

God is your deliverer.

That means He saves.

That means when you absolutely don't know what to do, when the crisis is so big, God has your solution. You have a hope. God's heart is set on delivering you.

David wrote in Psalm 22:4 (AMP), "Our fathers trusted in You; they trusted (leaned on, relied on You, and were confident) and You delivered them."

He then wrote in Psalm 34:4, "I sought the Lord and he answered me. He delivered me from all my fears." (NIV)

You might think that God rescues everyone but you. But that's not true! As you call out to Him, you are the one that will be rescued!

You are the one who will succeed!

God will put His fire extinguisher to each and every one of your fires — big and small. He will rescue you so that you are not put to shame.

THERE IS A SPECIFIC ANSWER FOR YOU

Deliverance in plain English means a solution. God has an answer for you. His heart is full of compassion for you. God's answers are not delayed; God's answer is action. When your answer is delayed, it just means that you cry out more to Him. A bigger answer, a better solution than you are expecting is about to happen. God works everything out for your good.

Keep your eyes open.

Psalm 71:23 says, "I will shout for joy and sing your praises, for you have ransomed me." (NLT)

The reason for the shouting is that the unexpected answer has come into reality.

Remember the time when you were promoted out of the blue? You shout when the unexpected comes your way. Shouting is a result of surprise and great emotion. You shout when you get a good surprise!

SCAMMERS: BEWARE!

My Norwegian friend Erik and I had gone to the dam, just outside the city. It was a nice place to pray early in the morning. I love to be out in nature, praying in a peaceful environment. We split up, agreeing to meet at a certain time.

Out from the trees, two guys approached Erik. They were very friendly. The two men kept admiring how tall Erik was.

Then one of the guys said, "Oh, you are so tall! I wonder if I can lift you."

He wrapped his arms around Erik's waist and at the same time, pulled the wallet out of Erik's back pocket.

The men immediately left. Erik watched them go back in the direction they had come from. He reached for his wallet – only to realize that he had been pickpocketed!

Erik came running. As we met up, he told me what happened.

We ran to the parking lot. The men had thrown a cloth over their license plate, and driven away down the steep sloping mountain road.

"After them!" I said in my bravest voice. We got in my car and gave chase.

And as we drove, pedal to the metal, we prayed to God who is our Deliverer!

We'll never catch up with them. It'll be a miracle if we do. I thought, as we drove down the mountain.

Psalms 60:5 says, "Save us and help us with your right hand, that those you love may be delivered." (NIV)

We continued to pray, not knowing what to do even if we caught up with the two thieves. We had nothing of any sort to defend ourselves.

The road was very windy. Cement barriers that were a foot thick were installed along the edge of the cliffs. As we came to the last hairpin curve – there it was! The getaway car - totaled!

This fairly new Fiat car had smashed into the concrete barrier. The front end of the car was completely crunched.

The thieves had fled on foot. We called for help and the park officials soon arrived on the scene.

As we stood talking, a tow truck came to get the car. When the tow truck owner requested permission to load the totaled car, the Park officials said, "No. We're not releasing this crashed car. The police are on their way."

Soon, the police found and apprehended the two thieves who had stolen Erik's wallet. Erik got his money back, as well as his credit cards and Norwegian ID.

How confident we were of God's love!

APPLE OF HIS EYE

When your enemies try and escape with your money, don't give up hope. When the credit card company is milking you for all you are worth – keep your head up.

God is loving and kind. God is merciful. This also means He fights for you. God always fights for the underdog and the oppressed.

Even if you brought the trouble on yourself, that doesn't affect God's response. The Bible says that you are the apple of His eye.

Deuteronomy 32:10 writes, "He shielded him and cared for him; he guarded him as the apple of his eye." (NIV)

That means that God is happy with you. He is pleased with you. Hey! He knows you are trying and calling out to Him for help.

KEEP TRYING

And when you love someone - you protect him or her. When you love your wife, you protect your wife. When you love your children, you protect your children. You protect what's valuable to you.

And you are valuable. God loves you so much that he sent Jesus to die for you - not to condemn you. There is no condemnation against you. But there is wild and abundant love for you.

God is certain to protect and deliver you, because you are a person He created. His care and compassion are evident in His deliverance. When you're coming home late at night, when you're driving alone, when you feel so lonely at school - God looks out for you.

DON'T BE A TRAFFIC MANIAC

My two kids and I were headed to the mall. Joy and Josh were excited! We were going to get ice cream, and then pick up some things for Mary Jane at the grocery store.

Driving down the road, an elderly woman and her family stepped out into the traffic to cross the busy road. I jammed on my breaks. The driver behind me was furious that I had jammed on my breaks to let the pedestrians pass!

The rules of the road in Turkey are: give way first to trucks, buses, vans, cars, herds of sheep, and last of all - people. I guess the other driver was running late, not feeling very courteous, or maybe in a bad mood or something.

He pulled into the other lane next to me, rolled down his window and began to yell at me and curse!

"You stupid *$#%! foreigner! Don't you know that you can't

stop for every *$#%! person that wants to cross this *$#%! road!"

This driver stopped his car right there in the middle of the road and yelled at me some more. And while he was swearing, a car came up from behind and rear-ended him! Smack!

Shocked, he then stopped shouting at me. He got out of his car, saw the damage, and began shouting at the guy who had just rear-ended him. My kids tried not to laugh, but they couldn't help it.

"Dad! Dad! Did you see that? That was like cartoons!"

After coming back from the mall — we again saw both cars. They were still there in the middle of the road, fighting it out and trying to sort it out with the police.

LOOKIN' OUT FOR YOU

God is looking out for you. He likes nothing better than to defend you, stand up for you, and make sure that no one abuses you. He cares for you, and even when you don't do everything exactly right — His heart is for you.

"Mercy triumphs over judgment." (James 2:13 NIV).

That means that you get good breaks that you don't deserve. You will be shocked with His protection. You will have a safety shield set up around you. As you are loved on, you will learn to value yourself. You feel good about yourself because you are defended.

God will pay back those who abuse you. Don't think for a moment that they will get away with it. You might not see the whole picture now, but I know that God doesn't keep a blind eye to abuse. He will stand up for you — even if no one else does!

TURNING OUT THE LIGHTS ON YOUR ABUSERS

We were traveling late at night in the eastern part of Turkey when our car broke down.

Smoke billowed out of the front hood. We coasted to the side of the road and I jumped out. It was pitch dark. And there we were, in the middle of nowhere. There were no streetlights.

In every direction that we looked, all we could see was... well, nothing. I looked under the hood, but couldn't see anything wrong. I had to squint to even make out the different car parts.

It was so dark! We locked up the car and hitchhiked back about 5 km to a gas station. By this time it was about 11 o'clock at night. We needed to find a tow truck. At the gas station, we explained our need to some guys loitering around the little store.

One guy offered to drive us to a nearby village. But he wanted such an exorbitant price to bring us. We were shocked! It seemed almost enough to hire a helicopter, or maybe even a jet!

We were at a complete loss of what to do. Dismayed, we left the gas station. As we walked off the gas station parking lot, I prayed.

I said, "That's not right. Lord, have mercy on these people who are trying to swindle us in our time of need. Our car is broken down, and we don't even have a place to stay the night. They are taking advantage of us. Lord, have mercy."

As I prayed, we walked away from the gas station and back to the empty road. Stepping off the parking lot asphalt, I swung my hand backwards.

And as I gestured, I said the words, "Lord have mercy." At that exact moment, the whole gas station went dark, completely dark.

Two minutes later, a little bus full of smiling people stopped and offered to take us for free to the next village.

As I got in the little bus, I was still trying to digest what had just happened! I was awed!

Sitting back in the bus, I was stunned at what had happened. God really does care for His own children. I felt my shoulders go back, a smile come on my face, amazed at how God would stand up for me.

I could just imagine the people in the gas station, scrambling for a match and trying to figure out what happened to their fuse box!

WHO TURNED OUT THE LIGHTS?

Can you imagine! Your steps are guided. There is a Shepherd who watches over your every move. I'm here to tell you today that God stands up for you!

In every difficulty, in every struggle the jury has already come in.

You will be protected! You will come through! In fact, He's already there. He's already protecting you. He's already defending you. Open your eyes and see that you deserve to be protected.

You might not see it, but that doesn't mean you won't get out of your situation. Go to the Lord.

God doesn't like abuse. He wants you to know that you are protected. And bad things just cannot happen to you without His stepping in. Your deliverance is near. There is hope for you yet.

God is kind towards you in your trouble. He doesn't treat you as others would. When other people try to take advantage of you, God won't let them get away with it.

He rolls up His sleeves and defends you. You can trust Him. I dare you to give Him an opportunity.

And if you do - you'll not be let down.

CHAPTER 5

LOVE WILL HEAL YOU

The first time I met Murat, I liked him immediately. Working at the front desk at a hotel in his small town, everyone loved Murat.

Sitting in the lobby, I couldn't help but notice the various exchanges.

"Hey Murat! We have to go for coffee sometime," one man said as he came through the revolving door.

"Hello Murat. Do you have change for a hundred liras?" a young woman asked. "Thanks, you are such a sweetheart."

"Murat, are you coming to the get-together tonight? Everyone's coming," another man quipped.

He must know everyone in town! I thought.

I met Murat through our Alo Dua Prayer Hotlines that we had established in four different cities. He would call in every so often and the team would listen and try to help him.

When he first called in, he had many questions. As his questions were answered, he made a decision and stepped out. He began reading the New Testament. He told us how his life was gradually changing for the better. And so he wanted to tell others. It slowly became known around town that he had decided to become a Christian.

One day, he and a friend were sitting in the local teahouse. Some members of the local political party walked in and motioned for him to follow.

"Hey Murat, come on over to our political party office. The head of the political party is waiting for you there," they said.

Murat walked into the office and sat down. He suddenly noticed the head of the political party, and four men advancing menacingly towards him.

"You dirty Christian. You infidel. We're going to kill you," one of them said.

Murat barely saw the fist flying towards his face. Punch after punch came at him. Murat screamed in pain, but nobody could hear him. The five guys had shut the office door and bolted it. There was no escape.

"You will renounce Christianity…" Whack. The main guy hit him over the head.

"…Or we will beat you." Whack.

"…Until we kill you." Whack.

The five men beat him until he was unconscious.

STILL BREATHING

Murat was finally found hours later, abandoned by his attackers who had left him for dead.

"Good. He's still breathing." The paramedics wheeled him into the ambulance. Bloody and beaten to a pulp, he was taken to the hospital and slipped into a coma.

Many people, began to pray for Murat. His story touched a lot of hearts. Everyone wanted to see him recover.

Murat remained in a coma for 3 months.

When he finally awoke, one could hardly bear to see his devastation. Murat could barely talk now, and his speech was slurred. They brought him home in a wheelchair. Murat's limbs would not respond to commands.

Murat's mother and father and his siblings were grief-stricken.

"How could those thugs beat him up like this? Just because he's become a Christian… That is the pinnacle of cruelty. Bigots! How could they destroy our son like this?"

IN YOUR DEEPEST PAIN

When you look back in your own life, there could be many reasons to succumb to defeat, or give in to bitterness. Sometimes we could go into an inner rage at our oppressors. We get angry against life and possibly go on a rampage of bitterness.

Why should I even care? Nothing good ever happens to me. I was cursed at birth. You give up trying and that destroys you even more.

You begin to hate life, hate progress, and hate taking promotion. Many times we subtly destroy ourselves. We begin to destroy friendships, family relationships. In so much pain, you feel you cannot get up from your pit of despair.

But in your deepest pain - God is there. How much more will He not freely give us all things (see Romans 8:32).

And today, God wants to give you all things - to take you out of your despair. He wants to treat you to good things, so that you heal from your hurts. God wants to take you out of your self-hatred and hardness on yourself. All the regrets, all the self-cursing will only serve to destroy you more. He wants to take you out of your destruction, and reverse your role from destroyer to healer.

You need a new spin on life. You are not someone who is destined to fail. You are someone who is destined to win. Stop being down on yourself. All you have to do is receive!

Receive that you are not a mistake. You are not a blight on the world. You are a wonderful creation of God. God created you with winning already on the inside of you. You were born to be significant. This is already weaved into your DNA. You cannot change that! You were born to do well. Will you receive His victory?

LOOK IN THE BLOODLINE

Why is it that when we go to a doctor, the first thing they ask is if the condition you have runs in your family? The doctors research and ask questions about your bloodline. Just as there are physical ailments that are generational, there are destructive habit patterns in our bloodlines.

I expect the Lord to bring healing in you right now. His love picks you up, because you are fearfully and wonderfully made (Psalm 139:14). He brings healing from the fear of rejection. He will free you from your subtle self-hatred. You are the apple of his eye.

The Bible says in Zephaniah that He sings over you (Zephaniah 3:17). He sings over you with love and perfect acceptance.

NOBODY IS PERFECT

We all know that our biggest enemy can be ourselves. Sometimes we use forgetfulness as a way to destroy. We forget meetings, opportunities, or we forget details that cost us friendships or financial loss. Forgive yourself. Nobody is perfect.

When you feel distracted or unable to handle your life, your finances, family, relationships, and work – please don't give up on yourself. It's not time to be disheartened. Everyone goes through some rough spots.

Sometimes we get sick because we need sympathy, comfort, and encouragement. This can be true. You are special and the unseen things you have been doing need to be noticed. You need to receive your due sympathy, comfort, and encouragement. And if no one else acknowledges that, I want you to know that God does.

Please don't give in to being sick.

Don't use the excuse, "Well, I get sick like this every year."

Or "Nobody cares if I get sick anyway."

Sometimes, the very reason you get sick is because you know that you are about to go to a new level. It's time for you to move forward, but you get afraid. You don't think you'll do well. More will be asked of you. So you conveniently get sick, so as to show the world that you can't receive the new challenges.

You need renewed courage for new challenges. You have the potential to do more, but often, hurts from the past keep you down. You might have failed in the past, but that is no reason that you will fail now. When you lack courage to proceed, just stick out your foot one step at a time. That is all it takes.

You might have seen your parents, knowingly or unknowingly, destroying themselves and the whole family's future.

Forgive your parents for the ways in which you saw them destroying. It's time for you to have a fresh new start in life. When you forgive your parents, their problems and shortfalls don't have to be yours too.

God has plans for your future. He's not out to make you squirm and fry like a worm under a hot magnifying glass. You are not disqualified from the dream God has placed in your heart.

So abundant life is not about just surviving. It's about trusting, and finding true answers, and happiness.

GOD IS A RESTORER AND HEALER

When Murat was released from the hospital and sent home, his family couldn't bear the pain and burden to see him the way he was. He was crippled and had regressed to acting like a child. His spirit was broken.

At times he would just burst out into uncontrolled laughter. His speech was slurred and he could barely walk. He couldn't work, only eat and sit around. He was bent over.

Murat's family asked if we would take him, so my church agreed. Together with another pastor friend of mine, we all set out to help Murat.

God is a restorer and a healer. Murat needed the confidence to face life again. We needed to find him a situation in which he could do well. We gave him the part-time job of caretaker in our office, and another light job of working for a restaurant.

Slowly, he would have to learn to be responsible, clean up, do dishes, and get along with the other staff. Everyday, he'd have to get out of bed, putting one foot in front of the other, and set out to face a whole new set of experiences.

YOU NEED FAMILY, THE KIND THAT LOVES YOU

This was a big challenge! He didn't know how to work! He still had to learn how to move his limbs again. But his faith was still intact. There was still a glimmer of hope in him.

And in his eyes, we were his family. He saw me as his father, calling me "Baba". He saw the other staff as his new brothers and sisters. We cheered him on every day.

"Murat, we know you well. We know that there's more to you than meets the eye currently. You are not a disability. You are a champion. You can conquer anything. You can do anything!" we'd tell him.

I NEED SOCKS

The first night that he stayed at the church, I gave him specific instructions.

"Murat, you must be quiet here tonight. You must speak softly. I don't want you to wake the neighbors," I spoke gently and clearly.

"Yes Baba. I will be quiet," he slurred loudly.

Two hours later, my cell phone rang!

"Pastor! Who's staying at the church?" I recognized the abrasive voice of our landlord. "Whoever he is, I want that guy out of there!" My landlord packs a gun, and at times entertains the police.

"Why? What has happened!"? I asked.

"Well, a lady from the neighboring apartment building called me. She said that a strange man stuck his head outside the window of the church."

"Well, that's okay. Sticking your head out the window isn't a crime."

"No. It's not what he did! It's what he said!"

"Well, what did he say?" I responded with a bit of apprehension.

"You'll never believe it! Of all the improper, rude, imprudent, inappropriate things to say to a woman."

Our landlord kept blustering on. I finally understood what had happened. Murat stuck his head out of the window, yelled to a lady in her balcony in the neighboring apartment building.

He shouted, "Excuse me, Mrs. Lady! Can you call my Pastor? I need him to bring me some clean underwear and socks!"

That was the end of Murat's stay at the church. We had to find him a permanent place to stay so he could always be with other church staff.

I BELIEVE IN YOU

The rest of us remembered how Murat was, before being beaten up. We knew his potential and that he knew how to work in a hotel. It pained us a lot to see him with his disabilities. But we could carry him because we believed in him.

We saw him as he was before. God sees you for your potential, not for your disabilities. He believes in you.

Many times Murat didn't want to work. He didn't want to do his cleaning responsibilities. He didn't want to do his therapy exercises. Actually, he didn't want to do anything at all. Being bedridden is easier than trying to walk everyday.

Many times, we just like being sick. It's easier to be sick than to do your therapy. It's easier to be sick than to keep fighting to get better. It's easier to give up on life.

But then, who can handle life? Who can handle all the things that life throws at us. People wound us – again and again. But then, just remember.

You have a specialist on your case. God is your healer. God is healing you.

"But He was wounded for our transgressions, He was bruised for our guilt and iniquities; the chastisement [needful to obtain] peace and well-being for us was upon Him, and with the stripes [that wounded] Him we are healed and made whole." (Isaiah 53:5

AMP)

Don't give up hope on yourself. Don't destroy your life by throwing down the towel.

EXCEPTIONAL IS YOUR NAME

You see you're really a special person. If I were to ask other people around you, they would tell me things that you can do well. There are things that only you can do well.

These exceptional qualities of yours need to be developed. Don't offer destructive excuses. I know you have more in you. Keep doing your best at work. Keep hoping to get better in your health. Don't justify your self-destruction by escaping life.

Jump in to God's arms, because He created you with a plan. He will fulfill the plan, as you trust Him. I want you to know that even the fact that you're reading this book shows that you are a person of exceptional courage, a person that doesn't give up. I know that because you are seeking the truth, you are seeking to become a better person.

You have courage, because you're hungry to do more with your life, and you haven't quit yet! You have a passion to dream, you keep on seeking the extra, and it is never too late for you!

BELIEVE IT OR NOT, YOU ARE CHANGING

Did you know that God is not bound by time? He uses time, controls time. He started by creating time. So any time that you might have wasted is redeemable in God's eyes. Any season of life during which you avoided success is redeemable.

Murat was changing. He was becoming more responsible, doing his work, doing his chores. He was getting healed. He began to walk better, walk taller. He was talking clearer and his slur had all but disappeared.

Why? Because he knew he was supported. He knew he was accepted. He decided that it wasn't worth continuing to feel bad for himself. He decided not to be bitter against his tormentors, the people who had treated him so wickedly. And Murat began to face life with a new passion.

But as time went on and Murat progressed, he began to be bothered that everyone was treating him as a normal person. He began to not come home at night. He'd wander the city, and we'd often spend hours looking for him.

And many of us are that way. You reach a certain level of success, and suddenly people begin to expect more from you now. But the fears begin to hound you back again. *What if I'm not good enough? What if I will fail miserably?*

And then we begin to destroy. We try to show everyone that we still need attention and that we need help. Talking ourselves out of succeeding, we find ways to destroy everything. We may begin to accuse people wrongly. Instead of seeing that we're the ones causing trouble, we conveniently blame someone else. It's time to face yourself.

You are the type of person that needs to succeed. So take a big breath, and just jump! You can do it. Don't destroy and go back. Don't listen to the fears! Because I know you can do it!

"I can do everything through him who gives me strength." (Philippians 3:14 NIV).

Time and time again, we wandered the city looking for him. We never gave up until we found Murat. Soon, Murat realized that we loved him no matter what. He was doing so well! He had gained a new confidence in himself, and could walk and talk again. It became evident that Murat was ready to go back to his family.

FAMILY REUNIONS

Family can be one of the hardest tests. Family can be great, but families can also destroy each other from the inside out. In each family could be cycles of destruction. Everyone has the same roots or propensity towards certain destructive patterns.

Being with family is a test that we must all overcome. That's why when Jesus healed some people, he told them to go back to their family.

"But the man from whom the demons had gone out kept

begging and praying that he might accompany Him and be with Him, but [Jesus] sent him away, saying,

'Return to your home, and recount [the story] of how many and great things God has done for you.' And [the man] departed, proclaiming throughout the whole city how much Jesus had done for him." (Luke 8:38,39 AMP)

Go back to the place where you are really known for who you are. It's a place where you cannot pull the wool down over the eyes of anyone else.

Being with family is a place where you will excel. You come face to face with your problems, deal with them and move on. Instead of hiding from who you really are – you can struggle through the pain and truth, and overcome!

You won't be able to hide. And your family won't allow you to hide. But it's your place of success. It is your place of healing. It's the place of overcoming. Looking in the mirror is not always easy, but at least you can start wiping the smudges off your cheeks.

Give to your family. In their healing, you will find your healing.

YOU HAVE OVERCOME

As you communicate the healing that has happened in your life, and tell them what God has done for you, your family can also receive healing.

No matter how great the difficulties seem, they can be overcome. One by one, and day-by-day, and hour-by-hour, you will overcome. Because God knows that you are one exceptional person. And he withholds no good thing from those who walk uprightly. He is making sure that you receive the good things.

God makes His goodness to pass in front of you. He demonstrates His goodness to us in front of our enemies. So much so that our enemies are put to shame (see Psalm 6:10).

You are one tremendous person whom God believes in! And I believe in you too! I know that step-by-step, you will change and see victory.

Don't beat yourself down so much. That's where grace comes in. God demonstrates His love to us, His exceptional power working in us. If the change weren't possible, He wouldn't tell us to do it.

His commands are good and it's possible to change.

The punishment has already been paid, so that we can change. Moment by moment, you are changing. He is absolutely for you. He believes in you. He is committed to you. And He never lets go. He is always forgiving, always loving. So hang in there.

You're actually doing really well.

STOP! 06 MA 985!

We were headed to a university in Eastern Turkey. After traveling many hours, we finally arrived. We had an appointment at the university campus with the library department head.

"Greetings! We've been eagerly awaiting these Turkish New Testaments. Our students will be thrilled! "

After drinking steeping hot Turkish tea, the Professor saw us to the door.

As soon as we got in our car, and drove to the university gates – I saw blue and red lights flashing and a siren going off!

"Stop! 06 MA 985! 06 MA 985! Pull over to the side of the road. Stop your car," the police car blasted through their loudspeaker.

"Uh oh. That's us. That's our license plate number," I thought.

We began to sweat.

One of our guys leaned forward from the back seat of the car and said, "Ian, what are we going to do? The trunk of the car still has a thousand Turkish New Testaments."

"Hey, don't worry. The New Testament isn't illegal, even if sometimes people think so. I have the court decision in my pocket. We'll just show it to them if we get in any type of trouble," I said nonchalantly (even though my heart was beating wildly).

I pulled over to the side of the road. One of the policemen got out of the patrol car and told us to follow him.

"But Mr. Police, I wasn't speeding. I was going 30 km an hour just like the signs say."

"You are being taken to the police station for another reason. Just follow our car."

We followed the patrol car to the police station. We were

marched into the police station.

"Sit. Sit down. You *speaky* Turkish?" they asked.

"Uh… yeah," I answered.

At that, the police began scurrying around the station. We were made to wait in the holding room. The air was tense. There was shouting; a ranking officer started barking orders.

Then we were marched into the room of a senior police detective.

The grilling began.

"Who are you? Who sent you? Why are you here?"

Another police detective stepped in.

"Who pays you?"

'Where does your money come from?"

"What government sent you?"

The grilling was hot! I was sweating. The bright lights hurt my eyes. I couldn't wait until they would let us go. I could hear my own heart thumping. In fact, I could hear all of our hearts thumping!

KEY TO UNLOCKING YOUR POTENTIAL

When you are under pressure, you begin to realize how excellently you can perform. The things that you fear and think will take you down - these are actually your next steps to success!

Stress and fear can actually bring the best out of you. You are about to do exceptionally well. The pressure and burdens that have come upon you are just what you need sometimes. They give you the extra push. This fear and pressure can actually promote you to the next level.

See the pressure for what it really is. Look at things from a positive light.

Isn't the pressure and stress actually helping you to perform with incredible skill, bringing things out of you that you never thought you could do?

And here you are… running as best as you can to accomplish the impossible dream.

God will take you where you are at and make a champion out of you! Fear and stress can even help to unlock your potential.

SHOWTIME: INCURABLE

After what seemed like hours, suddenly, the senior detective came in and said, "Okay, why are you REALLY doing what you are doing?"

He sat down and said, "Look, I'm really curious. What are nice guys like you doing way out here?"

Then he leaned forward and interrupted us. The detective lowered his voice and said, "Okay, I'm sick. I have a skin disease. The doctors can't cure me. I went through test after test. I went to see the specialists, and now, after eight years the doctors have pronounced me incurable. What about me? Will what you are saying work for me? Can you pray for me?"

I said, "Sure. Of course we can."

I was just about to pray, when in through the door burst another three plainclothes detectives. They were rough, stern men, with very piercing eyes. They demanded that we come along as they search the car.

They commanded and we obeyed. So all six plainclothes police detectives began searching every nook and cranny of the car. They looked under seats, took out the mats looking for secret compartments, knocked on panels.

LOVE IS SHOWN IN UNEXPECTED PLACES

While the car was being searched, the senior police quickly pulled one of our guys aside secretly and whispered, "Can you pray for me now?"

"I felt a jolt of electricity go right through my skin!" the senior police officer said excitedly.

"I'm extremely grateful," he whispered.

Radios crackled, we heard some talking. The police finished searching the car. Soon, we were told to get moving and follow the police car with its red and blue lights flashing. A second patrol car followed behind us.

They escorted us right to the edge of town and said, "Get out of town. And don't come back."

GOD WILL DEMONSTRATE HIS LOVE TO YOU

God showed His great compassion to the very policemen who were interrogating us!

In spite of the way we were treated, He healed the senior officer! I was thrilled in my heart!

God is a Father who loves all His creation. He loves the good and bad, the weak and strong.

He never stops loving, healing, providing, and giving second chances to you.

God doesn't sulk and disappear out of the scene. He continues to reach out to you and me.

God is relentless in His love for you. He continues to give surprises to you and me.

His love reaches out and doesn't stop – even to the downright rebellious, to the proud or hardened. He softens our hearts through His goodness.

"Or do you show contempt for the riches of his kindness, tolerance and patience, not realizing that God's kindness leads you toward repentance?" Romans 2:4 (NIV)

Today, recognize key times in your life when God has demonstrated His love and compassion to you.

And those times are not over!

There's more to come!

You cannot stop God from loving you.

DON'T STEREOTYPE

After four hours of driving, we finally arrived at the next city on our list.

There, at the university campus, we delivered the Turkish New Testaments to the head of the library. He was very gracious and kind. We again were shown the customary Turkish hospitality.

Different city… same story. As we stepped out the doors of the university, 10 plainclothes police immediately surrounded us. They seemed to jump up from the ground, drop from the ceiling, and come out from behind doors. We were in trouble again!

My heart sunk. *Does life have to be this hard?* I felt a burden of fear hit me like a ton of bricks.

The police demanded our documents. We handed our passports and licenses to them.

Looking at these detectives, I was intrigued. There was no way at all to stereotype them. Some of them were old; some of them were young. Some were heavy built; some were skinny. Each one was totally different from the guy beside him.

We were marched into a secluded area and made to wait for what seemed like days, but in reality was only hours.

The tension, the stress of not knowing what would happen to us was overwhelming. We could feel the suspicion around us.

I felt powerless. We were powerless. So we prayed.

Soon, I understood why we had to wait so long. They told me that we were waiting for the police chief.

Finally, the chief of police arrived with his entourage of men.

He took us into an office and interrogated us himself. This time, I was amazed because he was a very likable police chief.

Please don't misunderstand me. It's not that I wanted to get to know him anymore. I wanted to get out of there!

Anyway, it's nice to know that when people seem like bad guys, they could actually be the good guys. Just as I perceived that it is impossible to stereotype the police detectives, it is impossible to stereotype people.

After some more interrogating, they finally let us go. Imagine my relief as they gave us back our passports and licenses.

EVERYONE WANTS TO BE A GOOD GUY

People can be good and kind, mean or hard. Many times, there is a reason behind their problems. Give people a break because you are not in their shoes. And you don't know what they crisis they could be personally going through at this moment.

Everyone is trying his or her very best. Their best might not be very good, but it's still their best. You don't know what they are going through at home, at work, or with their extended family. So be easy on people.

Most important of all, give yourself a break. If you make a mistake, fine. If you ruin a situation, that's okay. If you mess up really bad, there's always tomorrow.

God is our boss in every situation. And He has an insurance policy that covers all of your mistakes.

He can turn any situation around, fix everything, and have you at the top in no time! He always works out everything for our good. When you love Him, when you are faithful to Him, committed to trusting Him, don't be hard on yourself or others.

"And we know that in all things God works for the good of those who love him, who have been called according to his purpose." (Romans 8:29 NIV)

REUNITED WITH OLD FRIENDS

I was so excited to head back home. However, we had a big, and I mean big, big problem. In order to get back home, we had to pass through the first city.

I didn't want to go back through that city, because the police had escorted us out of town. They ordered us to never come back. But there was no other route back home. This meant the necessity of traveling through the forbidden city again.

We thought perhaps traveling at night would get us through. This should be no problem.

Midnight came and went. We were still driving.

I assumed we'd be near the forbidden city in 20 minutes. I tried to relax.

Stop worrying Ian. Nobody is out at this time of night. It's going to be okay.

NO WORRIES, HAKUNA MATATA

However, my fears came true. A few kilometers outside of town, there was a police roadblock.

Past midnight, there were no other cars on the road. The police waved our car down. They shone flashlights in our faces.

"You *speaky* Turkish? You wait here," the one officer said.

I turned the engine off. We sat in the dread fear of night and waited for what could be harsh consequences.

Sitting there, I wondered why there was such a shortage of roads! All I needed was an easy alternate route! I needed a good break, but now it seemed that more trouble was coming my way.

The police radio kept crackling in the silence of the night. I tried hard to catch what was being said.

"Hey boss. We got them. Oh. Okay. Okay. Sure. No worries. We got it covered... Okay, we'll wait."

This part of the country has terrorist activity. I wondered if they thought we were terrorists or something? I didn't want my name to be associated with terrorists. I was just a Canadian that needed to get back home to my family and to a nice warm bed.

Waiting and waiting, the stress, tension, and fear seemed to be unbearable. After what I felt should be entered into the Guinness Book of Records as the longest wait in the world, we were still praying in the car fervently. The night was so still. I could hear the police radio crackling away.

I prayed, "God, please don't let the same police who kicked us out of town be the same police squad to come now."

YOU HAVE NEW FRIENDS

Soon, we spotted two police cars coming towards us at breakneck speed with their lights flashing. Six men jumped out and came towards our car.

I was terrified! *What would they do to us? What would happen now?* Thoughts flooded my mind. Even if we could, there was nowhere to run, nowhere to go at the sight of these six men marching quickly towards our car.

And lo and behold, they were exactly the same guys who had kicked us out of town!

They said in Turkish to the uniformed police who were manning the roadblock, "We know these guys!"

I wished for a case of mistaken identity. Maybe a helicopter could take me out of here?

Same scenario. One car drove in front with its red and blue lights flashing. Our car was in the middle. Another police car completed the entourage, lights flashing. We were moving fast in the pitch of night! I had no idea where we were being brought. It was two o'clock in the morning by now.

Oh home sweet home! I wish I could be there now. But it seemed that my official Turkish police escort would never end.

We drove and drove. I didn't know where we were. All of a sudden, we stopped. They had escorted us around the city to an unknown spot. What was next?

The police car in front of us stopped suddenly. I stopped my car. The police car behind us stopped too. All six rough and rowdy policemen jumped out of their cars and surrounded ours.

I was not about to do anything irrational at this point. But when I opened the car door, I was greeted by a handshake. These police detectives acted like they were our long lost relatives! The fear, the anger, the suspicion was gone from their eyes!

They had turned into friends! The police squad was so welcoming and so grateful because their senior police officer was healed of his incurable skin disease. You can't imagine how excited they were to see us!

GOD HEARS ALL YOUR PRAYERS

God made peace. God can take your most difficult situation and turn it into a blessing for everyone. There isn't just one piece of chocolate cake. There's enough cake for all, because God's heart is big. His heart is bigger than whatever you can ask or wish for.

When you are forcibly stopped along the road of life, and your prayers are not answered – it just means that we need to wait a bit longer before God paints the complete picture of what He is orchestrating.

He does hear those prayers. He knows the terror of feeling helpless by the side of the road. But He has other plans that are not just all about you.

God even cares for the police detectives who needed to be encouraged and built up and prayed for, even at two o'clock in the morning.

Just hang in there, because God wants to use you to add meaning and purpose to someone else's life. He knows that you are ready, because you have already been through your two o'clock in the morning. And He also knows it is about to be two o'clock for those you are about to meet and impact.

After all, you are God's creation. His plan for you is deeper and higher and wider than you can even imagine.

Many adventures await you!

CHAPTER 6

IMAGINE YOU: WALKING TALL

It was the worst time in years to sell our house. We had to move to another home, and we had to sell our old house right away! But the economy was struggling all over the country.

In our subdivision, there were at least 70 other houses for sale. The homes were all pretty similar in size and price range.

"Ian, that house has been for sale for 2 years," one neighbor pointed to a house on the same block. "They are selling it below current market value, just to get it out of their hands."

The whole area where we lived looked like a circus because of all the yellow and red "For Sale" signs. There were signs waving in the wind, signs hung up on walls, signs hung up on the street light posts, signs everywhere!

In order to sell our house fast, we would have to sell low and cheap. But I wanted to sell fast and high!

I was also concerned about who would come in and take a look at the house. As a foreign Christian Pastor, security is high priority.

Being on the WANTED list in Turkey did not help matters. I had been able to fly below the radar for a long time, and I wanted to keep it that way.

I was not about to endanger my family and myself. We had to go about this carefully. We discussed it so much that I thought I was writing a thesis called, "How To Sell your House While On The WANTED List."

THUNK, THERE GOES THE ROSEBUSH

It was extremely unsafe, but we needed to sell our house fast! We had been traveling for a few months and just returned to our home in Istanbul. It was about midnight. Dogs were howling at the moon and the neighbor's sensor security light kept turning on every time I moved. If only I could find the gate key!

I searched and searched through the luggage bags, feeling down into the deep pockets.

"I must have lost the garden gate key somewhere!" I thought.

After searching some more, I gave up.

If one way seems closed, there's always another route! Up, up, and over!

I heaved one luggage over the fence, then the next one. I took the third luggage, balanced it on my head, and then tried to throw it over.

Thunk! There went the rosebush my wife loved so much!

These bags are so heavy! I thought.

By the fourth luggage, I began regretting that we had brought so many chocolates from overseas.

The fence had spikes on top and was pretty high. Everyone had to climb over the fence. And then I jumped over.

We were in! So far, so good. I grabbed the house key, opened the door, and wheeled our luggage inside. I turned on some lights.

Hmmmm... everything looked okay.

I went downstairs to the basement. I reached for the basement light switch and stepped ankle-deep into water! Freezing cold water!

"Aaahhh! The basement has flooded!"

Well, we were very tired from the trip and needed to rest. The water could wait till morning.

I went to our bed and fell fast asleep. Within minutes, I heard Joy shriek! She called out to me from her attic room!

"Dad! Dad! Ewww...! Dad! Dad!"

I ran up to her room to see what all the shrieking was about. Well, it was obvious. Her ceiling was absolutely covered with thick green mold!

I thought, *This is bad! This is very bad.*

This was a perfect scenario for a poor me syndrome!

We helped Joy move into another room. The next couple of days were busy cleaning with the help of other friends. We used a water pump and covered our faces with masks. We didn't want to breathe in the mold!

After a lot of cleaning and sweat, the house was like new again.

I'm just giving you the light side of the story... It was a massive job. But I don't need to tell you all the sweaty details. The rest of the story basically was: scrub mold, don't breath it in, scrub mold, and drain out the basement, scrub, scrub, scrub...

LOOKING GREAT

There are times when we need to do major cleanup in certain areas of our lives. Hang in there! Even though the cleanup job is messy, you will look a lot better afterwards.

You might have dreaded the clean up job, but now the time has come. You can't procrastinate forever. Life is easier when things are cleaned up! You'll feel better.

That means having a clear conscience and a clean heart is very important. But don't be hard on yourself now. All you need is a little bit of change.

The difference between mediocrity and excellence is only a little bit. Your business may win a contract just because you tried a little bit harder. An Olympic athlete wins by percentages of a second. Drinking one extra glass of water everyday will do wonders for your health. And so giving of yourself to have things fixed in your life will make a load of difference later.

Take care of those pesky habits, and learn to relax so you can lower your stress level.

Let the cleaners go at it. You will look your best at the end of this short process.

Yes. You heard right, I said short process! You're going to come out of this looking great!

WHEN YOU'VE MISSED YOUR CHANCE

We were really hoping that the first people to come and look at the house would buy it. While I thought that was a good goal, I wasn't too sure of how it would ever happen.

We too put up our yellow "For Sale" sign to swing in the wind with all the other 70 houses for sale in our subdivision. And we waited.

Soon the first people to come and see the house arrived. They came as a family. The father, mother, and daughter!

I made small talk with them as we gave them a tour of the house.

"Ah! So you want to move to this area. To be perfectly honest, we think this is a good place for a family! You'll absolutely love it..." We talked as we went from room to room.

"So what do you do?" I asked politely.

That's when he dropped the bomb. The guy was the former local chief of police in our area!

I was very nervous! But I couldn't let on.

The chief only said two things. "One, I'll buy the house close to your asking price. And two, I really like your shirt. Can I have it?"

I thought well, *This is really the Lord's sense of humor. With all the arrests and harassments I've had with the police, the former local police chief is going to buy my house!*

But trying to be the best real estate salesman I could be, I said, "No thanks, we'll wait for a better offer."

I was feeling rather stubborn and told him I wouldn't lower my asking price at all. Not an inch! And I thought I might as well keep my shirt too!

But that evening, I did some research. I realized that this was an excellent offer and I had made a terrible mistake.

My neighbors told me, "If you get a buyer, take whatever offer you can get. Houses are just not selling in this economy."

I phoned the police chief up, and told him we would accept his offer. He responded that he was not sure anymore. His wife was interested in a different home now.

I was horrified! Here, the first people that had come to look at our house were ready to buy it – just like we wanted. And I had turned them down!

I went for a drive to see all the houses for sale – all 70 houses for sale in our area. I had just missed my open door and possibly closed it on myself.

We got down on our knees and prayed. We cried, and cried, and cried to God for mercy. We prayed until we filled a wastebasket full of tissues.

MERCY COMES IN

This is where humility comes in. You make a mistake and the only way to fix things is to be humble. The only answer would be if God miraculously turned things around for you. Mercy triumphs over judgment.

"I want mercy and not sacrifice. Go and learn what that means." (Matthew 9:13).

God doesn't want your hard work. He doesn't want your sacrifice. He wants to show you mercy. No strings attached!

I had to learn, and learn fast, about mercy that day.

Your intentions are great. Your heart is in the right place. You want to do the right thing, and you make some mistakes. Is there anyone out there with an eraser that does not just erase pencil marks, but erases mistakes in our lives?

Yes, there is such an eraser!

"Let us then approach the throne of grace with confidence, so that we may receive mercy and find grace to help us in our time of need." (Hebrews 4:16).

When you are so ashamed, and so embarrassed, He will cover for you.

Those who have never tasted mercy will say to you, "No! You have to eat what you have cooked up. What you have sown, you will have to reap."

Never mind those who have never tasted mercy. Just go for it! Take your case before God, be humble and ask for mercy. Mercy will come to you whether you deserve it or not.

When you have tasted mercy, you will know that you have tasted goodness.

You will forever savor mercy when you see it in action. And then you will begin to dispense the same generous mercy to others.

YOU WILL CLOSE THE DEAL

Then again, the police chief gave me a call. He said he wanted to meet at the IKEA cafeteria.

The whole haggling process began. The police chief drove up in his new car.

"Doc! I want to buy your house. How about I give you my car? In fact, I'll give you whatever car you want because I don't have a lot of cash available," I grimaced.

This was going to be a long day.

The police chief tried another tactic. "Doc, how about my son meets your daughter? That way, the house will stay in both of our families. My son is tall, dark, and handsome. He has a Masters Degree and is loaded with cash. He's my only son."

At that point, my daughter Joy started grimacing too.

We did meet the police chief's son the next day. He didn't quite fit the picture his father had drawn of him. And he was a boxer to top it off.

His buzz cut gave evidence to the fact that he had just returned from doing his military service.

After polite enquiries, the only response we elicited from him was a grunt. But later that afternoon, when I asked about boxing, he began to sing the "Rocky" theme song!

Munching on IKEA meatballs, the police chief said,

"You know we just can't help but come back to your house. We just love it. I'm willing to stand by my original offer."

We shook hands and agreed to meet at the bank at 10 o'clock the next morning.

I was especially excited because I had tasted and seen that God is good!

BRAVADO AT ITS BEST

But I had a dilemma. Because I was WANTED in Turkey, we didn't want the police chief to find out my name.

And of course I wasn't allowed to own land in Turkey. Helped by relatives to buy a house, we had put the house in my daughter's name.

During this time period, I had military detectives, special service detectives, and police detectives on my trail. They would come to the church, even attend the service, and harangue my staff.

Some would phone in to the Alo Dua Help Hotlines, asking to meet with me. Others would write into the website, pretending to be interested seekers.

So when the retired police chief asked my name, I said, "Just call me Doc."

You can imagine my agonizing worry. *What if he decides to do a background check on my family? What if he looks me up in the police database? And what if he gets tired of calling me "Doc"!*

In reality, it was pretty funny - but not at that time. He always introduced me to everyone he knew as "the Doc".

At one point, I realized the chief was getting suspicious. So I started leaving my ID in my car.

That sure came in handy. That very afternoon, the chief actually asked to see my ID.

The police chief said, "Hey, let me show my ID. Police IDs are very different than the normal Turkish ID." He showed me the way to tell a genuine police ID from a fake one.

"Now let me see yours!" He asked.

I gulped. I told him I left it in my car.

"Hmm…" was all he said with a suspicious glance.

YOUR CUSTOMIZED PROTECTION PLAN

One of the most well known Psalms in the Bible is Psalm 23. It says, "The Lord is my Shepherd… He guides me through the valley of the shadow of death."

You will come through every impossible situation into green pastures. He "will show Himself strong for your sake." (2 Chronicles 16:9).

"He will cover you with his feathers. He will shelter you with his wings. His faithful promises are your armor and protection." (Psalm 91:4 NLT)

That means that God has many ways of protecting you, hiding you, and bringing you through every unwelcome circumstance. He wants to make sure that you keep moving ahead and that you keep looking good. You are His kid, after all.

Right now, He is very pleased with you and your faith in Him. He is pleased with your attempts to please Him. Because you are trusting, He is making things work out for your benefit.

YOU WILL COLLECT

The police chief's bank was a different banking company than my bank. The teller at my bank said, "The best and most secure way to transfer this money is by armored vehicle service."

Wow! This complementary service came complete with one armored vehicle, two armed guards, and one machine gun!

The teller at my bank said, "We'll have an armored car come and pick up the money from the police chief's bank. Don't you worry. This is a normal transaction for us."

"Really?" I asked incredulously. "

I thought, *All this is going to be so exciting! An armored car, armed guards, and even a machine gun! Maybe I can ride in the armored car also. Or at least take a picture by it and put it in our picture album. Or post it on Facebook!*

It was not on my list of things to do, but it seemed exciting anyway!

IT'S A DONE DEAL!

After waiting a long time in the bank, the cash was ready. Our armored guards came in the bank. I had to give them a special password question. If they answered with the right answer, I would know they were the guards sent from the bank.

I had to go in a small back room and count the cash with the men from the armored car. One guard stood outside with his machine gun while we counted the cash.

Soon, the cash was zipped into bags, locked, and the guard quickly walked out of the bank toward the armored car with the cash! I panicked! There went the bags of cash!

I hurried out of the bank quickly, leaving the house keys with the police chief.

We put the money in bags and then the guards took the money and put it in their armored vehicle.

I thought, *This is incredible! I am on the WANTED list, and yet I just sold my house to the former local chief of police!*

I was extremely happy, because the deal was done, the sale was completed!

IS THIS REALLY HAPPENING TO ME?

Anyway, as I was saying, I was in a panic! In Turkey, a lot of transactions are still done in cash and not through checks. The bags of money were on their way out the door without me! I ran out the front door of the bank after the guard and his machine-gun toting buddy!

They put the cash inside the armored car. I got into my car, and prepared to follow.

The guards were about to pull out into the traffic, when an ambulance pulled up right behind the armored vehicle. The ambulance had its lights flashing and siren going. They parked literally one inch away from the bank's armored vehicle.

The ambulance attendants ran into the apartment building, and disappeared. We all stood there shocked!

Was it a set up? Was this for real? We were stuck! The armored vehicle was sandwiched in and could not move.

I thought, *What is this? What if this is an elaborately staged robbery? Is this some type of plot so that the ambulance personnel would steal the money? Would the paramedics turn out to be thieves in disguise? I think I've seen this in some movie...*

DON'T HURRY, DON'T WORRY

It was getting late. And we still had to drive to the bank, and deposit the money before the bank closed at 4 PM.

One of the armored car guards thought he would try and move the ambulance.

He opened the door of the ambulance, jumped in the driver's seat of the ambulance, and was able to roll it backwards. This was just enough room to get the armored vehicle out. Hooray!

As the guard was rolling the ambulance backwards, the ambulance driver came out of the apartment building! And was he mad when he saw the bank guard in the driver's seat! He was furious, hopping mad, about to start a fight.

THE CHERRY ON THE CAKE

Then, the second armed guard stepped out of the armored car with his machine gun. When the ambulance driver saw the machine gun, he quickly decided that if the guards wanted to move his ambulance - it would be okay with him.

The ambulance driver probably thought he'd better be a peacemaker real fast or get shot! He might be the one needing a ride to the hospital in his own ambulance! I am not sure, but we quickly got on our way.

We were glad there was peace. The armed guards got in the vehicle and began driving across town. We were in a second car, keeping up behind, trying not to be left behind at any traffic light. Actually we were not sure how secure our money was with these armed guards, so we followed really close behind them.

The guards brought the money into the bank, signed some papers, the money was counted and they left. They were very professional about it all.

So finally, our race of selling the house was finished! Now we're able to return our relatives' monies!

I took my yellow "For Sale" sign down from the roof.

And the cherry on the cake was that the house of the Christian Pastor was sold to the former local police chief!

SIT IN THE RIGHT SECTION

I have a Brazilian friend named Mario. He is a great soccer fan. When he took us to a soccer game, we were so excited! We waited in line for hours to get in. During the game, we cheered as hard as we could. Despite our loud cheering, our team lost.

In the soccer stadium, they sit the spectators in the section of the team that they are cheering for.

You do not sit in the wrong section if you want to enjoy the game. Some guys are bad losers. And then there are the types of guys that are really, really bad losers. You never know whom you might be sitting next to. So to enjoy the game – make sure you sit in your own section. This is for your own safety.

When the game was over, the fans of the winning team are allowed to go first out of the stadium. Because our team lost, we were locked up in the stadium for a long time. They had to make sure that all the winning teams' supporters were already out.

Our team's section was finally released when no harm could be done. The organizers and the police have found what would work best to prevent fighting among fans. This ensures that there is no violence after the football games.

You are on the winning side and the losers have to wait behind! You are free to run on ahead and keep in first place!

"The Lord will conquer your enemies when they attack you. They will attack you from one direction, but they will scatter from you in seven!" (Deuteronomy 28:7 NLT).

That means that as your enemies come after you, they will scatter. They'll become confused, disorganized, and no longer a viable enemy to you.

The result is mercy. In your last moments, when everything is flying wild, just hold on. Keep going because your deliverance is near. Your breakthrough is about to appear.

That open door that just passed is actually a revolving door that will open again.

The next section, the next turn of the revolving door brings another opportunity.

No matter what confusion goes on around you, hang on to your dream. Hang on to your vision. Hang on, because you are nearing the finish line. You are about to get the first prize!

You keep running the race - your race! Keep doing your thing, dancing your dance, and singing your song. Your heavenly Father is proud of you, and He continues to make a way for you to run even faster!

Just as God the Father said to Jesus, "This is my Son, whom I love; with him I am well pleased." (Matthew 3:17 NIV)

God says the same to His other children – us!

God affirms and builds us up. He lets it be known that you are his beloved son or daughter. No harm can come against you with an endorsement like that.

Keep running, keep winning.

Part II

Dream Again

CHAPTER 7

RISE ABOVE YOUR PAST

Many years ago, I was working a 9 to 5 job in Canada. I felt like it was utter drudgery. I had no purpose in the engineering department where I worked. All I loved in life was riding my motorcycle, a 750cc Triumph.

I thought, *What am I doing? I work to get a paycheck to pay my bills, to get a paycheck to pay my bills. There must be more to life than this.*

I finally came to the end of myself. I began a quest to study different religions, and researched each one thoroughly.

Pastor Tom was a friend of mine. He had a confidence and courage that attracted me to his life. Pastor Tom asked me if I wanted to pray together with him, but at that point I told him I was not ready.

One evening, I was in my house with my friends. I was drunk and was using drugs. I was so drunk that I could not stand up.

I heard a voice say to me, "Ian! You'll never be like this again."

I was not used to voices. That's for sure. I basically had grown up as an atheist.

"Ian! You'll never be like this again."

I heard that voice four times that night. I had a desire to get out of drugs, out of the lifestyle of partying and drunken nights. I wanted to be a better person. But you know how it goes. Good intentions don't always work out.

That Sunday I got up, put on my helmet and hopped on my motorcycle. I had made the very shocking decision to visit a church. They were very friendly and warm.

It was my very first time in a church. I looked around the auditorium, trying to soak it all in. At the end of the meeting, the Pastor asked if there was anyone who would like a big change in his or her life.

You're empty anyway. What can it hurt? You might as well try it even for a little while. I thought. *And if not, you can just go back to being an atheist.*

ENJOY THE SCENERY

Yes! I wanted a big change in my life.

Coming home, my friends asked me if I wanted to take some drugs. I answered no.

"Well, how about some drinks?"

I said, "No."

They began to laugh at me.

My friends mocked and said, "Why? Did they tell you at church not to?"

I told my friends that no one at church had said any such thing. It's just that all of a sudden, I lost my desire to drink and smoke.

The next morning, I got on my racing motorcycle. I was the fast motorcycle you see in your rear view mirror, and I'm gone. Everyday, I would drive like crazy to work. I loved to time myself and try to set a new record every morning.

That morning, I drove so slow to work. I enjoyed the scenery. I looked at the trees. I looked at the clouds. I kept wondering what was going on and why I felt so different.

I had so much peace, so much joy. At that moment, I knew that because I prayed to Jesus, He changed my life. I knew I was forgiven and could have a new start in life. A dream began to rise in my heart.

Now I would spend the rest of my life telling people about the good life.

TIME TO HOPE AGAIN

What's your dream? And what's hindering you? Is it your background, the way you grew up, the habits or decisions you made as a teenager?

I struggled a lot with drugs and drinking. My life was going in a downward spiral, faster than I cared to see.

No one believed I could make anything out of my life.

But deep down inside, I still had dreams of a happy life. All those dreams did come true for me now. But it wasn't before I learned to rise above my past.

You will too. Those dreams that have been lying dormant in you are still there. They have not disappeared.

It's time to hope again. It's time to believe that you can make a new start. God has put those dreams in you, not to defraud you, but to keep you moving forward to achieve those very dreams of yours.

In Hebrews 6:19 it says, "Hope is an anchor for the soul, firm and secure."

Hope doesn't disappear. It sits all the time, ready for action like timed explosives in a closet ready to go.

Proverbs 13:12 says, "Hope deferred makes the heart sick."

God knows your gifts and your talents. He put them in you. You are born for greatness. Your past doesn't have to disqualify you.

You can have a new start. And nothing you can do will change that. Even if you've failed again and again, you are still qualified to start anew.

It's time to let this hope in you explode!

CHECK YOUR TEXT MESSAGES!

Fast forward to Turkey. My beautiful wife and I were sitting on a park bench, gazing at the Marmara Sea and watching the sailboats. Joy and Josh were further up the beach, having gone to watch the windsurfers. It was a beautiful warm day, with a nice warm breeze.

We had fun eating our chocolate ice cream cones. Mary Jane and I just sat there and just enjoyed being together – sitting silently on the park bench.

Oh! It was good to just relax and enjoy my life. The seaside is definitely one of the perks of living in Istanbul. I never grow tired of it!

But all of a sudden, my phone beeped. I received a text. Pulling my phone out of my pocket, I glanced at it distractedly.

"No. No. I can't believe it! What is this?" I muttered to myself.

Mary Jane looked at me, alarmed. "What's wrong? What is it?"

We read the text message together. "There is danger. You will know who this is. Regards. You can reach me at 0577 358 8979 or 0594 724 0103 or 0562 449 5709. You can call me 24/7, 7 days a week."

We tried to decipher the mysterious message. There was no name on the text, and I didn't recognize any of the numbers.

"Oh never mind. Let's just get out of here first," Mary Jane warned.

We grabbed our bags from the park bench, waved at Joy and Josh, motioning for them to catch up with us.

I got up, just in time to see five policemen heading towards me. They stopped to check the ID of a different family who were picnicking behind us.

We walked the other direction. The policemen followed us. Mary Jane and I ducked behind a car. Joy and Josh joined us as we made our way across the seaside road.

"Don't look behind. Don't look behind. If you make eye contact, they'll tell us to stop. And we'll have to stop."

The four of us stared straight ahead, walking as fast as we could. I wanted to break out into a run, but that would seem too suspicious. The police weren't definite that we were their targets just yet.

I snuck a quick look over my shoulder. The police were still following us. They hadn't hopped onto their motorcycles yet, which was good.

We came to our car. We jumped in, and I pulled out into traffic. Weaving in and out of side streets, we all finally breathed a sigh of relief. We had lost the police, and left them still searching for us among the different families picnicking.

As we drove, my kids examined the text message closely.

"It looks like the message is from Bulent. You know, the old guy that comes to our church with his gun... and the guy we think is a secret service spy?" Joy and Josh said thoughtfully.

"Wow. He must have known about the arrest somehow. He must've been trying to warn us." Mary Jane exclaimed.

DREAM THE IMPOSSIBLE DREAM

Growing up, the thing I struggled with the most was fear. I was afraid at home, at school.

I didn't want my father to know how low my marks were. I didn't want to be the last one chosen to join the sports team. In fact, I was afraid of a lot of different things.

My fear almost kept me from pursuing my dreams. But I'm glad I kept going. It's been quite a ride ever since!

God will use you to do exceedingly, abundantly, above all we can ask or even think (Ephesians 3:20). So dream the impossible dream! And then do it.

You will end up with even more than you could imagine. So dream big! Because God's dream for you is even bigger.

YOU ARE ON THE RIGHT TRACK

Your dreams and visions are perfectly suited for you, for your personality, and for this time. Your handcrafted, tailor-made dreams are exactly what God has in store for your future. They are not a matter of if, but a question of when.

You are loved by God. He is totally pleased with you. Don't

think He is shocked by what you've done, or even by the lifestyle you lead now. He is forgiving. God is not hung up on your faults.

Jesus paid the price, so that you and God can be on speaking terms. And you can be put on the right track again.

Let this love of God renew your hope. Let it renew your passion for life. Let it renew your zeal. God's love will renew your excitement. It's time to rejuvenate your delight in life.

The hope is what keeps you fired up. It keeps you ignited and helps you to never give up. Although you might not think so, you actually have a deep hunger inside of you. Otherwise you wouldn't be reading this book.

And God is about to carry you to new heights. He actually delights in teaching you. Because when you meditate on what God says about you, everything you touch will become a success (see Psalm 1).

God has not created you for mediocrity. He's made you to pass with A+. He is giving you tremendous courage. His heart is completely for you. Receive His acceptance. His love is so high, and so wide, and so deep for you that it cannot be stopped. So pick up your hope.

Just run!

You can become number one.

HELLO, HOW CAN I HELP YOU?

I remember when we first opened up the Alo Dua Prayer Hotlines in the year 2000. It was right after the big earthquake of 1999 in Turkey.

Thousands of people had died in the earthquake, and the nation was still reeling from the pain.

We opened the Prayer Hotlines in 4 different cities – Istanbul, Ankara, Izmir, and Mersin, with a network of 25 Turkish churches across the nation.

As we advertised Turkish New Testaments in 8 different national newspapers, people from all walks of life called in.

Some of the callers were suicidal; other callers were on drugs. Young girls who had just gotten pregnant would call in. Housewives whose drunken husbands beat them would ask for help.

Everyday, we were receiving over 100 phone calls from people all over Turkey.

YOU CAN FIND AN ANSWER

Neslihan called in and said, "After you prayed for me, my addiction to painkillers disappeared. What happened?"

Our whole Turkish team congratulated Neslihan.

Hilal wrote in, "I'm a very angry person. I hurt a lot of people's feelings. After I blow up, I am very sorry and I try to pray to God. Please pray for me that I will have a patient disposition."

I told Hilal that it's a very big step to recognize his problems. As he becomes aware of the roots of his abuse, we will be continuing to pray together for complete healing.

"I'm proud of you Hilal. You are going to overcome!" I said.

Semir said, "I'm fed up and was considering becoming an atheist. But my friend gave me a New Testament. When I read it I wanted to believe. I now believe in Jesus. Your office called and prayed for me. It helped a lot. Thank you. I want to come to church. Is there one in Antalya?"

We connected him to the right people, so he could be helped.

Kemal called in and said, "Since childhood, I've been interested in Christianity. I read the New Testament. And I want to go to church. Pray for me that all my emptiness will be healed. Thank you."

Kemal came and visited our church in Istanbul. When he first came, I couldn't imagine him ever cracking a smile.

But as he continued to come, I remember the first time when I heard Kemal laugh so loud. That was a very good day. I could tell his heart was healing.

Selma from the registry office said, "When you give out New Testaments, you are loving people. Thank you for loving me."

Ozturk wrote in and said, "I'm thankful for the people who are brave enough to give out New Testaments."

Emir said, "Thank you! It's better to give out the New Testament so that people who can't afford one can read it. Let's help everyone! You've sure helped me."

THE SEARCH IS ON

Sometimes in attempting to reach your goals you might have things come against you. You might even have people try and stop you.

For many years, we've been going to Big Island in the Marmara Sea off the coast of Istanbul. Twice a year, our team would go to the island to pray for people during the bi-annual festival.

We started using a speaker system and microphones to preach in the open air and pray for people. Eventually, we started doing this at other locations as well.

Where do thousands of Turkish pilgrims go, and try to get answers to their prayers? Right there, on Big Island. Thousands of pilgrims walk up a long cobblestone road to a hilltop Greek Orthodox church. On the way up, they are not supposed to talk and must only pray to God for their needs. They tie ribbons in the trees, and some people even walk up the cobblestone road barefoot.

Every year, we'd pray for people with broken dreams, with sicknesses, for hurting families, and for those in financial turmoil. In a day, our team could even pray for up to two thousand people.

In two or three days, we'd give out anywhere from 3,000 to 13,000 New Testaments to people who really want them.

YOU ARE HIDDEN

As the team headed to our usual spot, three plainclothes police suddenly appeared.

"We are police," they said, flashing IDs. "Line up here, right in front of us."

"First of all, we need to find Ian. Where's Pastor Ian?" they asked my team.

"Pick up the phone. Call him." the police commanded.

Trembling, one of my guys tried to call me. "The call is not going through," he told the detectives.

"Let me see," the police grabbed the cell phone from his hand. "Uh-uh. You're right. No signal."

One of the guys on the team said, "He's here on the island. He should be here any minute now."

While the police were interrogating the team, the reporters would show up.

"Where's Ian? We need to find him. You have to tell us where he is." the reporters pried.

My guys were getting worried. With no way to contact and warn me, how would I know I was walking straight into a lion's den…

When you're in a situation where you think the wrong people are looking for you - that's okay. You will be hidden and covered. God is our hiding place. (Psalm 32:7).

You will become invisible.

The Bible says God is our high tower and our shield (Psalm 144:2). That is good enough to get you through your problems.

Yes you! Not little old you, but very special, highly important, much loved you.

DON'T PANIC, BE HAPPY

When I arrived on the island, I had no clue that the police and the reporters were looking for me. I didn't realize that the police were combing the area, trying to find me to arrest me.

I went directly to the teahouse with one of our guys. We sat there and discussed about some of the details for the event. We planned and prayed, and also drank tea.

The team couldn't reach me to tell me about the police.

While I was in the teahouse, the police went searching for me up the hill. At the same time, the reporters went up the hill to look for me too!

When I finished my tea, I too went up the hill. My associate and I slowly climbed, not realizing that the police and the reporters were up ahead. The police and the reporters never dreamed I was walking steadily behind them.

As I neared the top of the hill, immediately my phone started to ring!

"Ian! Everyone is looking for you... the police... the reporters... even I can't find you!"

"Whoa! Slow down. Take a deep breath. Start from the beginning. What's the panic?" I asked

"I don't have time to explain. You have to get off that road," the team member said.

As we spoke, my associate and I quickly walked off the main road into the forest. Within 30 seconds, the police walked by. And within two minutes, the reporters came running past as well.

The police never found me that day.

But I did run into the reporters later that afternoon.

They accusingly and angrily said, "Look, there's the head missionary!"

I knew that they were looking for someone to interrogate, so I just kept walking. But they followed me.

Huh? Are they still behind me? That's when I kicked into action and lost them in the crowd. It's like I just slipped right through them.

At the end of the day, we all caught a ride on the ferryboat and headed to mainland Istanbul. As the boat made its way towards the city, I thought about the beginnings of my time in Turkey, about my struggles with fear. I reminisced about how God has carried me through the terror and ongoing danger.

My team told stories of the day - of the thousands who had received New Testaments and prayer. Sitting there on the ferryboat on my way home, I remembered my past, and I dreamt my future.

KEEP LOOKING UP!

The Lord had hidden me! When you go about your job – nobody can stop you. When you do what you are gifted to do – nobody can stop you. And when you do what only you can do – still nobody can stop you!

You are special! God makes a way to keep you on track, to hide you from those who would try and hinder you from your goal.

God knows your past struggles. He knows that you might not

have done well in school. He knows you are still hurting from your divorce. He knows that you were abused as a kid. He knows it all.

He knows your very predicament. You've done so well by sticking it out. He is actually very proud of you, as you rise above your past!

He is working out everything for your good because you love Him.

P.S. He loves you too.

CHAPTER 8

DO YOUR LITTLE BIT

The road in front of our door was a mud hole. And when I say muddy, I mean slippery, really slippery mud. My wheels would spin in the mud, and we'd all have to get out of the car and help push. For three months of each year, it was an unusable road.

Our muddy road was a big problem. We couldn't bring groceries in that way. We couldn't park by our door. We couldn't even drive up to our door.

Trying to solve our problem, we threw gravel in the mud. We threw rocks in the mud. We threw boards in the mud. But somehow, it seemed that everything we threw in the mud just sunk down into the bottomless mud hole.

I had tried my very best. We had used up all our ideas. My son Josh and I had worked hard. We had worked long hours. But the road just kept getting muddier and muddier.

When you're not able to come up with any more solutions, when the finances are gone, when your relationships have seemingly turned cold - God has many answers for you.

You have used your initiative, your time, and your finances. You are not condemned.

Condemnation is not a spiritual gift. It is not anything that will help you or motivate you.

No Olympic runner has ever said in gratitude, as he receives his medal, "To my coaches! I want them to know how thankful I am that they constantly condemned me. Their condemning words have made me the fine athlete that I have become."

Don't open the door. Don't give any time to being down on yourself. You've thrown your rocks on your road. You've tried to be responsible. You've tried to be innovative. And you've used up your muscle and your sweat.

Your problems will be solved. Everyone knows how you've already done a lot. You've had to work hard to keep your heart clear of bitterness.

So let's not strive. There are other answers. When you look to God, the sun will rise. The clouds will shift. Your time will come.

WE TOLD GOD ABOUT OUR MUD

We spoke with the man who was the chairman of the community league. There was a fee that each household paid every month for the maintenance of the area.

"Please, can we do something about our road. The mud is making it very difficult. We can't even drive to our door."

The chairman just looked at us.

But the following week, he withdrew money from the community fund, and then proceeded to hire a tractor and buy gravel.

We were so excited! The tractor drove down our muddy road. My kids waved at the tractor driver. But the tractor kept on going.

Down the road, we could see the community league chairman as he directed the tractor where to place the gravel on the road. Hands on his hips, he kept shouting angrily at the driver.

"No! Put it right here! I said, put it right HERE!" the chairman ordered.

Instead of spreading the gravel on the whole road and in front of our door, the chairman of the community league ordered the tractor driver to only spread the gravel on his part of the road, by his front door!

But not in front of our door! Not on our side of the road! We were horrified! This was so unjust! The fund is for all the homes, not just for a select few.

We all pay into the fund, and how come they are using the fund for themselves alone? We thought.

We had many questions, but decided to just let it go. Some fights are not worth fighting for. We prayed and told God about our mud.

YOUR ROAD IS READY

What's next? We went down to the city municipality office.

They ushered us into the office, gave us some tea, and the whole staff gathered around.

"We have a mud problem on our road. Please, can you help us?" we asked pleadingly.

We explained our situation, and asked if the city can speed up our application to have our road paved.

Half an hour later, we walked out of there with a promise that they would pave the road within days.

That was easy! I thought.

And three days later, four trucks were lined up outside our house with a paving machine, and everybody was ready to go.

The road crew paved our muddy road. And they turned it into a beautiful paved street. The electric company came and installed a streetlight. And soon, the city even gave our road a name!

Our neighbors on the other block came to look. They were amazed. They had been waiting for 2 years to get their road paved. They wanted to know how we got our road paved so quickly.

God puts everything together. He'll pave your road!

We were so happy to have a paved road. All our neighbors were all amazed! They wanted to know the secret to getting a road paved. They were impressed. We were pleased to show off our new road.

Good things happen to build you up and give you confidence. Take time to think of the good things that have happened in your past. Remember your victories. Enjoy them, savor them, and let your past stories give you more courage to continue.

The Bible tells a story about a man named Moses. He was an Israelite. All the Israelites were slaves. But Moses had a dream to set his people free!

Moses complained, "God, I am ill equipped. You found the wrong person for the job. I stutter."

But God said, "What do you have in your hand?"

"All I have is a stick. This is my walking stick." Moses replied.

But it was enough! Moses was enough! God used Moses and his walking stick to perform miracles that terrorized and traumatized the land of Egypt. The Egyptians finally let the Israelites leave. Over two million people walked out of Egypt – free!

God was right. Moses did have what it takes.

And so do you.

EXPAND YOUR DREAM

As we expanded the book distribution companies, I was always on the lookout for other outlets to distribute books, always on the lookout for more national and foreign people to join us.

I started opening bookstands with Turkish brothers in various cities around the country. Forming teams got the work done. Networking with at least 25 churches around the country, the work began to grow and we've seen over half a million New Testaments distributed. Whenever I traveled, I took people with me so they could be empowered and motivated.

When you man a bookstand, there are certain things to know that will come in handy. First of all, wearing lots of layers of clothes will keep you warm. Always bring a hot drink in a thermos. And be prepared to stand out in the street for hours on end in the cold, sometimes rain, and even snow!

Some days, it was so cold that we'd take turns at the stand. One of us would go into a warm store and stay there a while. Then we'd change places.

There were a lot of people interested in the books. This was quite a season of risking. People weren't used to seeing foreigners on the street. One time, the police arrested us twice in one week!

"We'd like you to come with us. You are under arrest. Pack up your books. NOW!" they'd command.

I missed supper a lot those days. Every time I was late for supper, Mary Jane would get on her knees, praying for protection.

Joy and Josh would often plant themselves in front of the TV, watching the news to see if the book fairs had any trouble.

"Mom! Mom! Come quick! The religious festival is on the news." they'd call out.

Mary Jane would come running, and the three people that I love most in the world would cry out to God to protect the team. Then they would also call and inform other people for support.

GET A GPS

I remember coming home after a week of traveling. Then I entertained my family with the following story.

"I was in an Eastern city. We couldn't find the store that had ordered the New Testaments. I asked a taxi stand where the bookstore was. They gave us directions to the store.

When I walked in the store, I realized that the taxi stand had given us directions to the wrong store. The man behind the counter had a long beard, and didn't look very friendly for sure.

'Foreigner, what do you want in my store?' He was pretty angry. When he saw the boxes of New Testaments, he said,

'Get out of my store! Or I will blow your head off!' he yelled. "Out! I said out!"

We said, 'Oops! Sorry. Wrong store.' and backed out of there as quickly as we could.

So we left right away.... And that is the reason, my children, that you should always buy a GPS! Even taxi drivers can send you to the wrong place!"

DON'T GIVE UP

We would travel to libraries, universities, and second-hand booksellers, and donate books all over the country.

One professor would write us every year, requesting New Testaments for the whole class to read. We would visit prisons and donate Scriptures.

Joining book fairs, the New Testament would always be the most popular book in the whole fair. We usually had a crowd in front of our stand. I enjoyed seeing the expression of glee on young people's faces.

And at times the organizers of the book fairs wouldn't want us to join. But we always got our permission papers.

We constantly had to develop new strategies. We did over 20 different types of programs - open air preaching, prayer outreaches, festivals, internet, counseling tables, door to door survey, etc. The whole Batikent area of Ankara was entirely canvassed by our staff going to every home.

New Testaments were given out to every single person who requested them through our co-workers in different cities – whether by phone, email, mail, or in person.

We took to the streets and surveyed parks, shopping places, universities, busy streets, etc. We would give out thousands of New Testaments in just a couple of days on the city streets of Turkey.

Day in, day out, we would be at it. Frankly, it was also just a lot of hard work. My file at the police station got thicker and thicker. It's not always been easy for my family and me. I've now been arrested and harassed by police and military over 50 times.

GOD IS SYMPATHETIC

You get up early. You put in a little extra effort to stay up at night. You have a flash of genius and begin to scribble out new ideas – you are relentless!

You have dreams to get out of debt. You work on being healthy and disciplined. You want to bring your new business strategy into reality. In your heart, you hold specific dreams for your children.

I want you to know that God collects all your tears in a bottle.

"You keep track of all my sorrows. You have collected all my tears in your bottle. You have recorded each one in your book." (Psalm 56:8)

Be kind to yourself. Let's be sympathetic to one another's weaknesses, struggles and conflicts.

So when God sees you continue to struggle against your sin - day after day, and year after year, He is sympathetic. He will give you the strength to be healed of your addictions. And He'll bring those solutions.

He is not by any means a hard God. Straight away, He swings you up to His shoulders. He carries you.

DON'T LOSE HEART

As I distributed New Testaments and traveled all around the country, it first took 3 years to get out 5000 New Testaments.

We slugged on, day after day. And from there on, the doors started opening up. We began to see more opportunities come looking for us.

And as we passed the half a million mark, the newspapers wrote article upon article about our New Testament distributions.

"Virtually every person who has become a Christian in Turkey has done so by first reading some portion of the New Testament."

The Bible says, "Don't despise these small beginnings." (Zechariah 4:10 NLT)

It's your small beginnings that make up the end result. Without any small beginnings, there would be nothing to show at the finish.

Don't look down on somebody else's small beginnings, whether they are starting a home business, or if they are working two jobs to get out of debt, or trying to finish their post-secondary education. Most important of all, don't belittle your own small beginnings.

Your faithfulness will suddenly snowball into bigger things!

Every ocean is made up of tiny droplets of water. You were a small beginning.

And now, your small endeavors can multiply.

So do not lose heart.

CELEBRATING CHRISTMAS

It was time to hold our annual Christmas New Testament promotion. With around 20 people, we would present our gifts on the main streets of Istanbul, Ankara, and Izmir for 10 days. Having received all the official government permissions, this is how we celebrated Christmas!

One Turkish poet wrote, "And now because of the Christian workers, we in Turkey are also celebrating Christmas. They stand on the street corners, giving out New Testaments, and now we decorate our streets for Christmas."

As I stood in the shadows, monitoring my team giving out the New Testaments, three plainclothes policemen stepped in from nowhere.

"Pastor, we are here to protect you today. Have you had any problems?" the three plainclothes detectives stuck out their hands, introduced themselves, and then took their position around the street. The most inconspicuous men I'd ever met – these guys really knew how to blend in. They were good!

For ten days, thousands upon thousands of New Testaments went out in Istanbul, Ankara, and Izmir.

One group worked at the church from morning to late evening, putting contact information in the back of the New Testaments. They would order pizza and work without breaks, so as not to disrupt the workflow. Those guys were unstoppable!

Simultaneously, three teams were distributing on the main shopping streets of Istanbul, Ankara, and Izmir.

THE FAMOUS BOOK

Our Christmas event attracted the attention of Rahsan Ecevit. Rahsan Ecevit is the wife of former Prime Minister Bulent Ecevit. In 1985, while her husband was in jail, she founded the socialist party DSP. Bulent Ecevit was finally released from jail, and went on to become the Prime Minister of Turkey.

She does not wear a headscarf, is one of the few female

politicians, and is a driving force in Turkish politics.

She is the type of politician that when she has something to say, everyone listens!

She and her husband Bulent Ecevit made a statement that got the newspapers, the TV channels, the magazines, and the forums into a media frenzy!

"We are losing our religion. New Testaments are being given out on our busiest streets! Soon we will be losing our country. Everyone will start wearing crosses from their skull caps!"

YOUR PHONE IS RINGING OFF THE HOOK

As soon as they made their statement to the press, our church phones, our Alo Dua Help Hotlines, and even my cell phone began ringing off the hook.

After the New Testament promotional event, I headed to the church. I couldn't believe my eyes. Reporters were camped out on the corner, waiting for me to arrive.

"Pastor Ian, good to see you. See those reporters over there? They've been waiting out here for three days." my neighbor friend pointed to them.

"Look, you'd better be careful. How about taking the side road to the church?" he continued.

I turned around and made a beeline for my car. I headed home, ate supper, and then returned to the church after nightfall. I slipped in the side entrance, and bounded up the flights of stairs.

As I unlocked the church door, I noticed that our sign had been broken down and smashed. I quickly stepped inside.

But wait!

There was a noise coming from inside the office.

I crouched down and silently moved across the church to the office.

I could hear a voice shouting.

I walked in the door of the office, and located the voice! It was coming from the answering machine.

For about half an hour, some guy kept the threats coming on the answering machine.

EVERYTHING WORKS OUT FOR YOUR GOOD

But God works out everything for good to those who love him. (Romans 8:28) The attention in the media grew to over 1000 national newspaper articles about our New Testament distribution efforts! They publicized our Alo Dua Prayer hotlines, our church address, and our phone numbers in 3 different cities!

And without any help at all, the New Testament promotional events had gone viral!

People were discussing the New Testament distribution all over the place. From the internet forums to the guys in the teashops – everyone hashed and rehashed the topic.

Huseyin wrote an editorial on the topic of New Testament distribution saying, "We are very poor nationalists. We are not very hospitable. Even if we are a 99% Muslim country, and there's one person who wants to be a Christian, why does this cause such an uproar? Now I understand why we are not joining the European Union. There should be freedom for all religions."

Alp wrote an article in response to Rahsan Ecevit's statement saying, "If we Muslims want to convert or read the New Testament – there should be freedom to do that. Don't pressure me to stay in any religion. If I want to explore other religions, I should be free to choose. People should not be ostracized from society if they change their religious beliefs."

Mert, another editor wrote, "Muslims can open mosques or TV stations, or give out Korans in Europe. So why can't we let Christians practice their religion in our country. Why is there opposition?"

THE SNOWBALL EFFECT

And then everything just snowballed from there. Some authors wrote about New Testament distribution work in books. At least 4 poets wrote poems about our distribution teams.

Hack teams routinely received hack requests for them to take down our site. Media began reporting on the New Testament distribution events we do.

A religious foundation was also created to distribute free Korans in response to our New Testaments. Sometimes, we'd be giving our books side by side with them. This was actually really nice – a true picture of people getting along.

An Islamic Prayer Hotline was formed in response to our Alo Dua Prayer Hotline.

There were direct complaints that Korans were so expensive to buy, and yet New Testaments were being given. The newspapers would exaggerate that the Turkish government allocates funds to buy free Korans to distribute! We'd see banners along the road advertising free Korans.

Such rumored big operations were certainly a bit overkill compared to our small team of people. We didn't always have the manpower or the funds, but the media and government sure thought we did!

Freedom of religion is paramount for a society to grow and flourish. People from all over the country began writing in, requesting a New Testament from us. We received a lot of letters saying thank you.

They would say, "Since you distribute the New Testaments with full government permission and police supervision – this gave me the courage to go out and read the New Testament. It has changed my life."

TAKE ANOTHER STEP

Sometimes you might not see the results of your small efforts right away. But small rocks are what make up a big dam. That dam later goes on to produce hydroelectricity.

When you speak out your dreams, no matter how small they begin, they will become a reality. As we confess our dreams and take small steps, we have the power switched on.

God rewards those who diligently seek him. Just hang on! It will come. Just take another step today. And remember that God is absolutely for you.

The Bible tells a story about a man named Nehemiah.

Nehemiah's home city was in ruins. Nehemiah wanted to rebuild the wall. That way, the city's enemies would not be able to come in and plunder the city, taking all that they wanted.

Nehemiah was an important official in the King's Court. The King asked him what he wanted. At that moment, he prayed a small prayer. And the King gave him money, soldiers, and all the legal documents that he needed.

In the end, Nehemiah built up the wall of Jerusalem in 52 days. A true record!

Keep your small prayers going up to God. He hears! And he loves to answer. He is merciful to you. He is generous to you. He is patient, loving, and kind. He opens up new doors for you and he does miracles.

YOU ARE SIGNIFICANT

God will take the little that you know, your little amount of money, a little amount of experience, and make it significant. God will add to it and multiply it.

Your work will be reproduced and increased.

Sure, you might not have enough experience. That may all be true. God looks at you as a person. He doesn't look at what you don't have.

He doesn't factor in your education, the amount of money you have in your pocket, and your family background when calculating His love for you.

In fact, God doesn't calculate His love for you.

He just gives it all.

CHAPTER 9

YOU DON'T NEED TO LACK

Bang! Bang! Bang! Someone was hammering our door down. The team members peaked through the peephole. It was the police!

The police came in the door, swung it shut behind them with a loud thud. The police grabbed one of our personnel by the neck and slammed him up against the wall.

The police shouted, "Where is Ian?"

With the hand squeezing his neck, Arif could hardly even answer.

They stormed into my office, gathered up the team, herded them into the kitchen, and set a guard at the kitchen door.

In order to pacify these men, my daughter Joy timidly sneaked out from the kitchen to serve them our special Belgian chocolate cookies. When they saw the cookies, the police let Arif go.

He weakly slid to the ground, while the police ate the whole tin of cookies.

They sat down at my desk, started smoking cigarettes, and prepared to camp out waiting for me. Soon, I arrived. As soon as I walked in the door, I smelled the cigarette smoke.

"Get out of my chair. And take your feet off my desk. I don't allow anyone to smoke in my office," I said loudly.

The police jumped. I guess they hadn't heard me come in the room. They hastily complied.

I took my turn sitting at my desk. They asked me many questions.

I said, "Everything is open here. Here are my records. Here are my books."

The police said that there had been a complaint against my company that I was money laundering. I called our accountant and told him what was up.

He said, "Just show them the books."

These police are actually from the commercial division, and they're trained accountants as well. They looked through the books, made copies, wrote a report, drank some more tea, and cheerfully went on their way. We were cleared!

A well-circulated urban myth is that we put $100. bills in each New Testament. The Turkish newspapers claim that this is true. It certainly is a wild thought. It sure would be something to give out thousands of dollars just like that! But it certainly isn't true.

Sometimes, people will come up to me on the street and ask if I have any of the "Books with $100 bills in them"?

I'll jokingly reply that I took the $100 bills out to pay our electric bill at the church.

YOU ARE AN OVERFLOW PERSON

Many times, you might feel that lack is your only friend. Being in situations of lack may be all that you know. But the truth is, you don't have to constantly be in a position of lack.

God is generous! Let's receive from His big heart. You were made to be a receptacle of God's blessings.

It is not God's plan to keep you in a position of lack. But He does want to move you into a position of having the ability to help the poor. God wants you to be big-hearted today. There are a lot of hurting people in the world, and each one of us can make a difference.

Rationalizing that it's okay for you to stay in lack can be rather selfish. You need to have extra so that you can give to others. You need to have more so that you can have the right tools to work effectively. You need to have the surplus so that you yourself can be motivated to help others.

God wants to meet your needs. Just like a father enjoys giving his children presents at Christmas – God enjoys giving presents to you! Do you need health, your relationships to turn around, or maybe a better job? He desires to supply your wants and needs. Because God is open-handed. He gives.

Goodness is a major part of God's personality. Being good also means being a liberal giver. He provides, He blesses. Our lack is an opportunity to taste and see that God is good.

And when you have tasted and seen that God is bountiful, you become kindhearted to others. And the more good that is demonstrated in this world - the better things are.

WIN THE LOTTERY

One day, I walked in the Alo Dua Prayer Hotline office. The entire team had a smile on their face.

"Hey everyone!" I greeted them. "What's happening? What's so funny?" I asked.

"Well, today a lady named Fatma called in. She said, 'Look. I'm going out to buy a lottery ticket. Please pray for me that I win the jackpot," Deniz said.

"And Abdullah here said to her, 'Of course I'll pray for you to win. Just remember to give to our church when you win,' " Deniz continued.

We all looked at Abdullah. He still had a big grin on his face.

Continue to trust the Lord for His provision to you. This is your season to move on to blessing. You can have lots of joy, which you can give to others. Or else you might have insights that you can help others with.

As you see and take stock of your life, you realize that you have received in many areas so that you can pass it on to others.

Encourage others. And when you know and understand how good God has been to you - radiate it wherever you go. In your home, workplace, and school - make it a part of you to radiate God's goodness.

You are a change maker because of all that you have gone through and all that you've seen.

Take time to realize all that God has done in your life - so you can encourage, build up, and empower others.

I'M SO PROUD OF YOU

Serhat received a New Testament from us in one of our street outreaches. He read the New Testament, and decided to believe in Jesus.

Serhat said, "I believe because the New Testament is a Book of love."

Serhat came from a large clan of terrorists. His parents abandoned him when he was just a little child. Serhat's uncle brought him up.

At a young age, he became a guerilla fighter in the mountains. At a young age, he was caught and spent some years of his life in jail.

Serhat was in his mid-twenties. But he started to understand true love. We watched as his life was slowly transformed. He became secure in the fact that God loved him.

Slowly, Serhat became more confident. He began to relate to others and talk more. He stopped acting afraid and timid.

What you need most is love. Just think, *God loves me.*

One day, Serhat came running into the church. "Pastor, I am so glad to see you! I just got kidnapped and I escaped...." Serhat began talking, his words running into each other as he tried to explain.

"Whoa! Slow down Serhat. Here, take a seat," I said as I pointed to the couch. "What happened to you? We've been wondering why you weren't at church."

"Pastor, you know how my Dad has been so angry that I became a Christian and left the terrorist organization? Well, he sent two of the terrorist thugs to kidnap me. They dragged me into an alley, blindfolded me, and took me to a boat dock."

"Serhat, are you okay. Did they hurt you?" I asked.

"Oh, I got scratched up a bit. But when they took off the blindfold, I began praying – just like you do Pastor. I spread my hands up in the air and yelled, 'Jesus! Jesus! Save me!'

At that very moment, the two thugs started shaking. And I mean, their whole body was shaking like crazy. I didn't even take time to stare. I just turned tail and ran. And that's why I'm back today, Pastor!"

"Wow Serhat! You are growing in courage and strength! I'm so proud of you," I smiled with relief on my face.

PERFECTLY LOVED

God is aware of our desperate need for affection and affirmation. He is the only one who can love us perfectly. To be loved perfectly means to be loved no matter what you do. There are no popularity polls, grading reports, or evaluations. You are loved perfectly. It is that simple.

This whole world is seeking for love. We need love in our families. We need love in our workplaces. We need our friends to love us.

You are someone who deserves to be loved. Your mistakes and flaws are not taken into account because you can be forgiven. And God has chosen you to be someone that He fills with His perfect love!

And when you are loved perfectly – that means you can ask God for His best for you. Make out your concern list! Nothing is too impossible.

Like we say to our kids, "What do you want for your birthday?" Ask yourself that question.

What would make you happy? Don't be afraid to ask God about your needs.

HEY SWEETIE

Another year, I was beat up on the street when we had the New Testament stand. And boy! Did it hurt!

Some months later, I was summoned to the courthouse. The judge sentenced me to jail because of being a Christian Pastor. But an old friend of ours offered to pay the bail instead.

Joy with some of the Turkish team walked down the long corridor of the courthouse. In front of them, a man in handcuffs was being marched off to jail. Women were crying. Men huddled in little groups, with worried expressions on their faces, waiting for their friends or relatives' court cases to conclude.

Our team later told me how they were so afraid. They asked for directions, and finally found themselves in a large room filled with men with moustaches at computers.

"Hey sweetie! What's a nice girl like you doing in a place like this?" A big burly man leaned forward and spoke through the glass window.

"Sir, I've come to pay my Daddy's bail," my daughter stepped up to the counter.

"What did your Daddy do, sweetie?" the man inquired curiously.

The whole room went silent. All the men stopped tapping at their keyboards to hear my daughter's answer.

"Sir, my Daddy is a Christian Pastor."

DEPARTMENT OF JUSTICE

When my friend Kenneth paid my bail, his act of kindness showed me another facet of God's character. It was a large amount of money.

God doesn't want you to suffer and struggle. This is never God's will. He will make an easy way out for you.

God has seen all the injustices that you have been through. He saw that time when you were abused. And the time that guy swindled you – He'll take care of your costs.

Injustice can scream at you, but you don't have to carry

bitterness. God is in the department of justice. He works to ensure that His children get the vindication that is rightfully theirs.

He'll bail you out.

MY YOKE IS EASY

Jesus said, "Take my yoke upon you and learn from me, for I am gentle and humble in heart, and you will find rest for your souls. Come to me and learn from me. For my yoke is easy and my burden is light." (Matthew 11:29, 30)

When our good friend offered to pay my bail. That was my easy yoke. I could have refused to pay bail and spent more time in a Turkish prison.

I could've hired a lawyer and fought the court case. Some lawyers with the European Court even offered to take up my case. I felt that in this case, it would not be worth it. I would have spent years fighting it, end up with enormous legal costs, and lose a lot of sleep, and peace and joy over the case.

The ensuing publicity would endanger my family, my church, and my work of feeding the poor. It just wasn't worth it.

God has made your burden light today. You can walk with your head held high. Every yoke of guilt, shame, harassment is broken off you! God delights in looking after you.

Ask God for what you need. Don't try to stick it out and persevere in living a hard life. Of course there are times you have to fight and tough it out. You will have wisdom when to take up the case or not.

He's already paid your bail. Take the easy way out. God is kind towards you. He has all the resources to bail you out. You don't have to lack anything.

Just enjoy your bailed out life.

CHAPTER 10

YOU ARE BEING CARRIED

My son Josh and I were riding our bikes along the Turkish seaside. The skies were blue, the birds were singing, and the waves lapped at the big black rocks.

Our little puppy Mighty ran along with us. Mighty is small, but she runs faster than we can pedal. As we raced around the corner, suddenly our little 20-pound, bundle of energy named Mighty was attacked by two 200 pound dogs. The two dogs were huge shepherd dogs, mangy and rather emaciated.

A young woman desperately tried to control the two dogs, but the two dogs were too strong for her. She stumbled and fell on the gravel, losing hold of the leashes.

"Stop Bruno, Stop Alek! Stop! Stop it, you monsters!"

One of the dogs soon had our puppy Mighty in its mouth and lifted her up in the air.

Josh and I were horrified! We had to protect our little family pet!

We spun into action. Josh and I rammed our bike wheels into the dog that had Mighty in its mouth. Mighty was up in the air, trying to get out of the big dog's mouth.

"Alek, Bruno! Let the dog go!" The young woman was screaming.

Finally, the big dog released Mighty. Mighty limped away, whimpering. I picked up Mighty in my arms and we hurried away.

We have quite a few stories like this where Mighty gets attacked by the bigger Turkish dogs. Packs of lost or stray dogs roam the area. Most of the dogs are used as guard dogs, so they are very large.

Mighty became very confident around these large dogs. She forgets that she's little. She forgets her size. Mighty always thinks she is a big dog. She thinks she can handle any other hundred pound guard dog.

But you see, Mighty has always been protected and defended by us.

Mighty truly became the meaning of her name. She knew that somehow or the other, those big dogs would turn tail and run.

ALLOW YOURSELF TO BE CARRIED

When you are in crisis, know that Someone bigger is backing you up. You need to have the confidence that you will eventually overcome. You welcome situations that make you successful, situations in which you win and build confidence.

The dream that lies dormant in your heart is sometimes only ignited by desperation. I know you feel the pain of loneliness and the pain of the impossibility.

God knows that you have that dream. He knows your gifts and talents. And He's ready to put things together. But sometimes desperation is the key. Allow yourself to be cared for and carried.

The Bible tells a story about a man who was a blind beggar. His name was Bartimaeus. When blind Bartimaeus heard that Jesus was coming through, he shouted out, "Have mercy on me, Jesus!"

He kept shouting as loud as he could to get Jesus' attention. All his friends that had the ability to live a normal life told him to be quiet. But the Bible says, "Bartimaeus cried out all the more."

And that "all the more" part is really what you're made out of. Despite everything coming against you, you have kept going "all the more". And right now, "crying out all the more" is your gas pedal to get things really going!

Your sense of inadequacy, your fears, and those troubling weaknesses are actually stepping-stones for your success.

Take some time and try telling God about your problems. Maybe in a bedroom, maybe in your car, maybe outside somewhere – tell God what you are going through. Cry out and tell God.

Jesus heard him and sent for Bartimaeus.

Jesus asked, "What do you want?"

Blind Bartimaeus answered, "I want my sight."

Blind Bartimaeus was healed because he wouldn't stop shouting until he was brought to Jesus.

What do you want? Don't worry if what you need seems too big to ask for. If you need the impossible, if normal just won't cut it, and if you are feeling like you are at the end of your rope - those are the prayers of a champion. Go ahead and cry out. You don't need to wait any longer. God will carry your worries and burdens.

YOU NEED A PICK UP

At one point, just after the war with Iraq, we wanted to help in a practical way. The Iraqis were beaten down, destroyed, and hurting. Fleeing from their homes, they had left everything behind to try to get across the border to safety in Turkey.

The tent camps that they lived in at the border were far from sanitary, and fights for food broke out often. Rows of tents stretched as far as the eye could see.

We traveled by bus to a point that was about 20 km away from the Iraqi border. From there, we had to take the taxi to the border camps.

I asked around town and finally found the taxi that was running regular trips to the border camps. We put the boxes of supplies in the trunk of the taxi and got in with several other men who we did not know. Everyone was headed to the border.

We were all squished like sardines in the taxi. I had a hard time with my long legs. I tried one position, then another. I finally gave up on trying to find a comfortable position.

As the taxi driver made his way out of the parking lot, the tires were scraping.

I realized, *My boxes of supplies are way too heavy! I hope the taxi driver doesn't get mad and throw us out of the taxi! We'll end up on the side of the road. And soldiers are crawling all over the place. We might end up in a military jail.*

Scrape, scrape, scrape. The taxi driver stopped the cab in the middle of the deserted road. I anxiously scanned his face to see if he was angry.

He said, "Okay. We have to do something. Let's put all the heavy guys in front. Lighter guys in the middle."

Again we drove off, and the tires were scraping. All over the place, there were Turkish military roadblocks. I did not want the taxi to be stopped and searched.

I said, "Lord these are your supplies and we also have the New Testaments here. Please lift up the car."

And at that moment, the car tires stopped scraping. And we drove all the way to the Iraqi border!

YOUR CONCERN LIST

What concerns do you have that are weighing you down? God's love for you is so great! He has actually prepared good things for you. When you're at the end of yourself, and have run out of your own answers - the solution is already waiting for you.

When you take the time to cry out, He sees and hears your prayers. God will act on your behalf.

He knows that it is success that brings confidence. For when you see the answers coming your way, confidence is built little by little. You walk with a spring in your step and a new strength in your heart. And you pursue more! You are carried from stepping-stone to stepping-stone.

God is honored when you do well! Because it wasn't your resources, not your own strength, or your brilliance that brought your plans into place or your dreams into reality.

The Bible says, "Zeal for your house consumes me." Psalm 69:9 (NIV).

The disciples said to Jesus, "Teach us to pray".

"During the days of Jesus' life on earth, he offered up prayers and petitions with loud cries and tears to the one who could save him from death, and he was heard because of his reverent submission." (Hebrews 5:6 NIV).

Jesus prayed to God and cried His heart out. When we pour out our worries, concerns, and fears in prayer to God – we give Him our burdens expecting miracles from Him.

God enjoys fulfilling dreams. And He loves to ensure that the things you cry about are taken cared of. Because He does exceedingly and abundantly above all that we can ask or even think.

In the New Testament, Jesus tells the story of a shepherd who had a lost sheep. That sheep was totally unaware that it was lost or in danger. The shepherd left the 99 sheep on the hills, and went searching for that one lost sheep. He found the sheep, put it on his shoulders, and carried it home.

God hears your concerns. He puts you on His shoulders and carries you back home.

PROBLEMS ARE ONLY SYMPTOMS

In our office we had a diligent, lighthearted guy. Hilmi was always eager to help and work, although he had a lot of hurts. But Hilmi also had a serious problem.

"Ian, my father left us when I was a young child. I've floundered a lot in life. But I want you to know that I'm really excited to make a new start," Hilmi said.

As time progressed, a problem became evident to me. Whenever I would send Hilmi to pay a bill, he would come back and tell me I had given him the incorrect amount of money.

Many times, Hilmi wouldn't give back the right amount of change. He would confuse things and would always somehow change the facts. Sometimes he'd tamper with the bill, so he could keep part of the money for himself. I began to see that he was stealing in many different ways.

Hilmi was a great worker, except for this one problem. Perhaps you could call it being a thief.

So how did I solve it? We had a great relationship. But how could I teach him? So I just didn't let him handle money. He continued to develop and learn other talents instead. And over the years, Hilmi became very faithful.

I never let Hilmi handle any money, and he never had a problem with stealing money again!

My first instinct could've been to lay him off. However, I saw that his problem was only a symptom. He had great potential to do well, but had grown up in a small shack and lots of poverty. Life had been difficult, and Hilmi just needed someone to believe in him again.

YOU HAVE A GREATER PURPOSE

It was better to carry Hilmi, and help him to be successful. It was better to see him developed and become faithful, rather than to cut him loose.

It's time to admit to yourself that God actually cares about you with your particular problems and faults. Yes, He really does.

God sees the bigger picture for your life, and has a strategy to help you become more confident and successful. You are not rejected. He overlooks your problems, and works with you where you at, so as to see you successful.

As you are loved and given chance after chance – you will eventually realize there is a better way. You will be motivated to do your best.

When we realize that God trusts us and even carries us while we are sinning or rebellious – this is what transforms our heart.

God is bent on carrying you. It is God's character to carry. He's determined to help you.

Many times, we would like to translate our own images of our fathers, put it on God, and make Him out to be the heavenly police. We only see Him as a hard judge. God is both loving and strong.

LOCKED UP, BUT HAPPY

You just have to love the Black Sea coast! John, Howard, and I had traveled many hours to this city by bus. It was absolutely beautiful!

We had to deliver boxes of New Testaments to two different addresses. So after a good night's rest at the hotel, we split up. John and Howard headed to one store, and I headed to the second store.

Within two hours of leaving the hotel, Howard and John began to be followed by police detectives. As they made their way through the city, Howard and John had no inkling of the police lurking behind them.

After lugging the boxes of New Testaments, and delivering them to the specified store, Howard and John decided to head back to the hotel and join up with me there. We had planned on having lunch together at the café near the hotel, once we had finished our deliveries.

As Howard and John headed back, they came face to face with the police.

Howard took one look at the police and slipped into the shadows. He ran into an alley, and the police weren't able to catch him!

But they took John to the police car, shoved him in the back seat, and turned on the police siren. The police drove at breakneck speed to the station, pulled John out of the car, and locked him in the holding cell.

ARE YOU ALONE?

"Ian! Ian! They've taken John away!" Howard came running into the hotel lobby.

I called my wife Mary Jane to tell her the news. John is a

German national, and so she right away called the German embassy.

While this was all unfolding, the police interrogator began to work on John. They shone a bright light in his face and told him he'd better cooperate, or else!

"What are you doing in our city? Who sent you? Are you alone?" John bravely answered with silence.

"Are you alone?" they asked again. The police asked a third time, again a fourth time.

Finally, John cracked.

He opened his mouth and bravely said, "Yes, I am alone right now."

John was a faithful guy. He didn't want to go get Howard and I arrested also. But he was terrified.

Within the hour, the German embassy called the police in the station where John was being held.

The police walked into the holding cell, and said,

"You're free to go. But I thought you said you were alone. How did your embassy know where you were? But anyways, you can go now."

John came back to the hotel. We sat at the café and we laughed about his harrowing tale and narrow escape!

YOU GOT THE JOB!

It is God who is strong on your behalf. He carries you as a single mom working and trying to make ends meet. He carries you as a student working your way through school. He carries the family who is going through fears of house foreclosure.

One of the more painful prayer requests we had from the Alo Dua Prayer Hotlines was from a young girl by the name of Aysegul.

"My father tries to commit suicide. I don't know what to do. I'm always on edge, always trying to keep an eye out for him. I can't live with this stress all the time."

Aysegul would phone in for many days and ask for prayer, pour out her heart to us.

Then one day, after 10 suicide attempts, Aysegul's father killed himself. He eventually took his life and left a trail of misery behind him. Aysegul was so broken-hearted at her own failure to be able to stop her father and save him.

"Nine times I've saved his life. Nine times I was there at the right moment and kept him from killing himself. But now…" Aysegul just broke down and cried.

Now she was fatherless. She carried a huge burden of guilt.

"My father was the provider for our family. Now, I need to find a job. I'm so depressed, I can't even bring myself to go out of the house"

Aysegul would call and we would pray for her often. We prayed for her heart to heal and mend. We prayed for courage and for her not to carry that weight of shame and guilt. Aysegul had not been out of the house since her father's death.

I still remember the day that Aysegul phoned and said, "Guess what! You prayed and I was able to leave my house and go to the job interview. On top of that, I got the job. And it's a job I absolutely love!"

GET READY TO FLY

You were never meant to carry the horrific burdens of others.

You are created to be a success. You are not created to carry the burdens of your parents, or even the wrongdoings of others. God will carry your problems.

Carrying the burdens of her father and his attempts at suicide crushed Aysegul. It was too much for Aysegul. Being burdened down with guilt and shame is not what you were intended for.

Jesus said, "I came to set the captives free." (Luke 4:18) Do you feel captive to your problems, captive to your family's problems?

Being a captive is not what was intended for you. You are free!

You are set free at this moment, in the mighty name of Jesus from the stress and fear that is overwhelming you. You are set free from every wrong burden, every bit of guilt, and shame.

Allow the Lord to restore your joy, your vision, and your passion as He carries you.

You were meant to fly!

CHAPTER 11

EXTRAORDINARY WILL COME LOOKING FOR YOU

All our team was excited to head to Africa to launch our Africa event! We bought our airplane tickets and found ourselves already landing in Johannesburg. A big convention was happening in the city, and all the chain hotels were booked full.

So we all grabbed our luggage bags from the conveyor belt, and proceeded to head to the airport information kiosk.

"We need a place to stay in your beautiful country," I said to the people at the kiosk. They found some rooms for us at a quaint little bread and breakfast, with stuffed animal heads hanging from the walls. Our team joked about our inner hunting instincts beginning to surface!

Ahh! Clean sheets! And a place to finally sleep!

When we arrived at the hotel, we immediately hit the sack. The following morning, we had various meetings since this was a trip to train our Turkish team. From there, we traveled to an orphanage and began to learn about the massive orphan population there.

After our time in Johannesburg, we headed back to the airport to catch a plane to the next African country.

Arriving there, it looked just like the pictures. Women carried large containers on their heads, as they walked along the red mud roads. Everyone was dressed so colorfully.

The driver took us to the hotel. That evening at supper, we found out that there was a large number of disabled people staying there as well. Some had only one arm and one leg. Different ones crawled up the steps. It was very painful to see.

However we were able to strike up some friendships with various ones, and sat around laughing together. We really bonded with them.

They constrained us, "Come with us. Tomorrow is Disabled Day! There is a big gathering happening and disabled people are coming from all over the place. Even the President of the nation is going to come and address us. It will really be a celebration."

I said, "We'd love to come. We'll meet you tomorrow, bright and early."

CELEBRATING, AFRICAN STYLE

When we all awoke the next morning, at breakfast my daughter Joy said, "I had a dream about the President last night."

As the driver drove down the road, each of us was amazed. The streets were lined with people dancing and chanting, as they awaited the arrival of the President. Dump trucks full of singing men made their way down the road. From the smallest child to the elderly men - everyone was dancing. We loved it!

Then all the traffic was stopped, so that the President could pass. First came military trucks carrying soldiers, a cavalcade of motorcycles drove by. Then came four black cars full of the President's special security men. And finally – the President in a big black limousine!

More truckloads of cheering and singing supporters of the President followed the procession. Our driver pulled in, as the very last truck passed to join the line. We felt like we were in a parade.

We finally arrived at the celebration grounds - amidst the high-security. We met up with our new African friends, and they introduced us to different sponsors of the event and government personnel.

"Joy, be ready to tell your dream to the President if we get a chance." My daughter looked at me incredulously, but then she grinned.

"Okay, Dad."

The President arrived, walking down the red carpet with his personnel. The crowds cheered! About 20 plain-clothes security guards surrounded him. We were enjoying the ceremony.

The President was making his way down the red carpet when unexpectedly, he veered off the prescribed path. He began shaking hands with the crowd, and suddenly – we came face to face with the President!

WHISPER YOUR DREAM

Joy was frozen and I could see her knees were shaking, so I put my hand on her shoulder and she stepped out.

One of the men who was standing next to the President moved, and then we were able to slip into the inner circle of bodyguards. The impossible was happening! The guards turned, the President saw us. We moved forward.

Joy stuck out her hand and said, "Mr. President, I had a dream about you. God says to you… " For about 30 seconds, Joy whispered the dream in the President's ear. He graciously smiled and moved on, shaking the hands of the crowd.

Joy was exuberant! "Dad! Dad! I actually met a President! I told him the dream. I was so afraid, but I knew you were right there. You made me feel brave."

Our team was seated in the VIP box with all the government dignitaries. The whole event was very festive. They had special ethnic dancers and drummers come, and different people made speeches.

But despite the general joviality, I felt uneasy. I felt someone was watching us. Finally, I turned around. The bodyguard of the President was staring at us. He motioned at us.

Oh no! Not again! I didn't think we'd get arrested in Africa too! I thought.

"Give me your full names, your home address, the room numbers and the hotel address where you are staying in town. Also give me your cell phone numbers. I need your passport numbers too," the big burly bodyguard said.

We hoped we were not in serious trouble. After giving him all our information, we sat down again in the stands. Soon I felt someone staring at me again. I looked back. It was the same bodyguard. He motioned again.

"The President would like to meet with you," he said.

"What? Really?" I exclaimed. But then I remembered.

"I'm really sorry. Please accept our apologies. I'm not sure what to do. We're supposed to be leaving the country in two hours. Everyone already has their tickets and it will be too late to change our departure with the airline." We felt so downhearted.

What a missed opportunity! But the bodyguard had a solution. "Well, as soon as you reach your destination in Kenya, we will arrange a conference call with the President for you."

NO MISSED OPPORTUNITIES

We hardly had time to think before our driver whisked us away to the parking lot. We had to get to the airport.

However due to presidential protocol, no one is allowed to leave the grounds while the President is addressing the people. The President had just started his speech. The military security would not allow our vehicle to leave.

Finally we asked help from the President's personal assistant, and he told the military to release us and let us through. We hurried to the airport on the rough roads. We were still late.

The plane was still there, however they would not allow us on the plane. We had missed the cut-off time. We begged and pleaded, but no! They wouldn't allow us on the plane.

YOUR SUN WILL RISE TOMORROW

Perhaps you've thought about accomplishing a dream, and then got stopped. Maybe you've tried to keep that appointment to apply for better job, and then missed. Maybe you've quit dreaming even before you could take the chance.

Keep trusting that God is for you. Keep believing that God will direct your steps.

When you think the doors are closed, they are not.

The missed opportunity may not be missed at all. Maybe it just means for you to try again – just try the next door to your right!

You don't have to be anxious for anything. Believe in miracles, believe in the goodness of God.

Your dreams may feel squashed, but don't lose hope.

The sun will rise tomorrow, and joy comes in the morning.

MEET THE PRESIDENT

We tried so hard to get on that plane. The airline personnel just sat there, and shook their heads.

"No way. The doors are closed. If the doors are closed, the doors are closed," the lady at the counter said.

Our next step was to phone the colonel, the personal assistant of the President.

"Mr. Colonel! We missed our plane. We're still in the country. Will it be possible to meet with the President?" I said.

The colonel was very understanding and kind.

He said, "Yes, the President would like to meet with you. However, setting up meetings like this takes time. You must be patient. But we will make it happen although your whole team can't come. We have to limit the number of people to just you and your daughter."

I didn't think to bring a suit to Africa. It's too hot and sweaty. We rushed hastily to the center of town. Our host Jawara told us that most suits could only be tailor-made and ordered. Ready-made suits are rare and difficult to find.

However, we found one store that had a suit my size! It had been quite a challenge.

But wait! The pants still needed to be hemmed.

Oh well, we don't have time. Maybe the President won't notice. We'll be fine as long as he doesn't look down at my shoes.

As soon as we bought the suit, the Colonel phoned.

"In two hours, you have an appointment with the President."

YOU ARE READY, PANTS HEMMED OR NOT

You are the message. A tremendous door is opening for you right now - beyond your belief. Even if your pants are not hemmed up, you are really ready!

You have things to say and do that will impact society. The mundane things you do everyday are preparing you for greater levels of responsibility and service to others.

God is in control of your life. You might not be able to leave the parking lot. And you might miss the airplane. But you will be in the right place at the right time.

And no matter what – you will meet with the President! And he can give you information to empower you to help others.

What do you dream about? What makes you tick? What you are envisioning is exactly what makes you interesting as a person.

These are the things that will enrich the lives of others. Your gifts, talents, and personality were given to you for a purpose – so that you can do well.

Two guards with machine guns took our IDs at the entrance to the Presidential palace. We walked wide-eyed through the Presidential Palace. We hoped it wasn't obvious that we were shocked. The President's staff took us from one room to another room. Sweating and nervous, we were briefed on protocol.

Then, we met with the Colonel who once again instructed us on the proper protocol. We were ushered into the President's massive office.

Looking around a highly decorated room, we gingerly sat down on the gilded gold furniture.

The President walked in, and we stood up. His men backed out of the room.

We explained the dream to him, and began to pray for him. The dream was regarding an assassination attempt on his life.

"Mr. President, God is for you! God is on your side. God has chosen you to lead your country at this time," I said.

The President warmly welcomed us to the country and said to us, "You and your ministry work are welcome here."

ROYAL TREATMENT

You are very unique and you have a message. Your message makes you come to life!

And yet, it needs to be told to the right people at the right time. Your message is your purpose.

Please don't discredit yourself.

You have a lot in you.

Matthew 10:18 says, "You'll be brought before governors and kings for my sake."

That means you can also meet the leaders. In fact, you can become a leader in your field, your home, and your office.

You can be the very best you. This is part of the destiny that is on you.

We flew into Africa to do our work, not expecting that we would be given the royal treatment!

After that, everywhere we went — everyone tried to help us once they knew we had been to see the President. At the hotel, at the airport, with the local African Pastors that we had met — it helped our team to effectively minister in the country.

Use your gifting and your unique talents to get to the top of your field.

Your relentlessness and humility will pay off.

As you use your talents to serve others, they will not go unnoticed.

"GOD IS ON MY SIDE"

After we left Africa and went back to Turkey, an assassination plot was uncovered against the President. This was in direct line with the dream that Joy had shared with the President.

Many different people were arrested. The following day, the President made a state of the nation address.

The headlines of the national newspaper were, "President says in state of the nation address, 'God is on my side!'"

The very words that we had used to encourage the President were the ones he used to encourage his own country!

"God is on my side"!

GOT A SECRET?

God shares his secrets with His people. God is revealing to you incredible secrets that will help you help other people. Those secrets and ideas will cause a ripple effect, multiply, and can even make history!

Continue being faithful. Continue serving and doing your best. Those who serve well will advance fastest. The last in line will become first.

There are incredible days ahead of you! Continue to prepare yourself. Strengthen yourself. Build yourself up. This is your time.

Don't make excuses and don't expect delays. Don't give up! You are doing really well – just keep doing it. God is a rewarder of those who diligently seek Him.

YOUR GIFT WILL MAKE ROOM FOR YOU

Week after week, we faithfully held church services. I studied for sermon after sermon in Turkish. At first, we only started with our own staff. But word began to go out about our church in Istanbul.

One Sunday, reporters secretly filmed our church service. Our church service became the top news in the nation! For three days, the national TV news program played 20 minutes of our service on the six o'clock news.

They put it on loop! We'd turn on the TV and see ourselves on the news! This brought a lot of publicity among Turkey's 70 million 99.8% Muslim population.

For most, it was probably their first time to have seen or virtually attended a Turkish church service! The whole nation of Turkey was able to watch a Turkish church service first-hand!

All of a sudden, we were nationwide! Different pundits, Islamic theologians and even psychiatrists came on the news talk show to discuss our church service. Reporters from other channels camped outside the church for days, hoping to get an interview.

YOU ARE NOT ORDINARY

We are all different, but God has made you to be exceptionally you! Do what you are best at. Do what you enjoy, and what makes your heart happy.

It may not always seem glamorous, but keep on being you. Day after day, as you serve others – you won't be left out. You will receive your own breakthrough.

What you do everyday might seem so normal. But other people watch you, and are amazed with the ease that you perform your tasks. You are good at being you!

You have many skills. And what you are doing will grow. All your perseverance will eventually pay off. Congratulations! And as you become even more determined to better yourself, it will show.

As you exercise your skills and faithfully give of yourself, you will not lose out. Life may seem pretty normal. But your turn will come!

You are growing, developing, changing, and adjusting things in your life. Everyday, you are being compassionate, kind, merciful, and serving.

Keep going. Keep serving. Keep giving. Some days, it may be hard. You might feel lonely. But you are not alone.

My friend Yuksel called me up. "Ian, the news channels are calling me. They want to interview you. They promise prime time and will allow you to say whatever you want."

"You know, I'd love to. But I have to keep on with my work, there's lots of doors opening," I answered on the phone.

News reporters showed up at church and camped outside, waiting for me to arrive. Our church received many requests for interviews. I turned them all down. That just added to the furor! The media dubbed me as the "007 Missionary".

"Pastor Missing" was another headline. The reporters were trying their utmost to flush me out.

For us, holding church services was normal. It's what we did every Sunday. We would pray for people and minister to people. But to the rest of Turkey – they found church to be something strange and amusing! Never seen before!

OUR DOG MIGHTY: PUBLIC RELATIONS DEPARTMENT

After our church service was shown on TV, we received a flood of phone calls, emails, and letters. We were so busy! Other news agencies wanted to set up interviews. We rejected all requests for interviews. Everyday, a new story broke out about our ministry work!

We needed a break from all the stress. Life is not all about work; you need to have fun. So our family and staff headed to Pizza Max – one of our favorite places to eat. Even our dog Mighty came along for a ride in the van.

We left Mighty in the van and tromped in the door of the pizza place.

"Hey! Welcome guys, welcome to Pizza Max. Long time no see." the waiters were so friendly and hospitable.

We all sat down at a big table, and ordered our pizza. But then all of a sudden, the restaurant became still. Everyone was staring at us while eating pizza. We tried to unobtrusively eat our meal, but I could still feel all eyes on us.

"Beeeep! Beep! Beep! Beep!" Everyone looked out the window at what was honking. It was our dog Mighty! She had gotten into the driver's seat of the van, put her paws up on the steering wheel, and leaned on the horn.

"Beeeep! Beep! Beep! Beep!"

The whole restaurant erupted in laughter. The silence and tension was broken. The other customers came over to our table, said that they recognized us all from the news.

"Pastor, we want you to pray for us."

So we were happy to interrupt our pizza to pray with people. They were struggling with many different concerns. They needed a compassionate and listening ear.

And our dog Mighty bridged the gap! Creating a humorous situation, everyone felt at ease to tell us their pain.

WE NEED YOUR TALENT

You have something that other people need. It might be a talent, a skill, knowledge, or even the ability to make others laugh. To you, your gift may seem insignificant. But let me assure you. We all need your gift.

God will take your gift, and make it prosper. You will do well in your family, your reputation, and it will even affect your finances. People who you need to meet will come into your life. Because you've been faithful in developing yourself and your gift, greater opportunities will come looking for you.

You dreams will come true – as a result of your dogged spirit. Just keep doing what you know is right, day in and day out. Keep doing what you know in your heart you have to do.

It may be hard some days, - but don't lose heart. Because your gift will surely make room for you.

DR. IAN HERINGA

Part III

You Are Loved

DR. IAN HERINGA

CHAPTER 12

YOUR HOLIDAY IS WAITING

It was a sunny day, the perfect day for a picnic. A few of us packed a picnic lunch, and we headed out to the forest. Time to relax!

We had a great time eating together, talking, and laughing. We threw the ball around a bit, ate sandwiches, and enjoyed the sun.

Piling in the van, we turned on some music, and with heads bobbing to the cheerful music – we headed back to our office.

Out of nowhere, a car came speeding alongside us. He tried to cut us off as he pulled ahead of us, and stopped his car in the middle of the road.

He jumped out of the car, and ran towards our still moving van. I tried to maneuver our vehicle around him, but he started banging on the window of our van, trying to break the glass!

I drove up on the sidewalk, drove around his car that was blocking the road. I put my foot on the gas pedal, pushed it all the way down to the floor.

I got to get us all out of here and to safety! I thought.

The extremist got in his car and began chasing us. He had recognized us from the TV news program, and was giving chase.

I turned into a side street, and then drove through an alley. The van's tires screeched.

I zigzagged through some different streets.

Finally, three minutes later, I said, "I think we lost him."

But no! At the next corner, we spotted him again.

The extremist saw us too! And he came at us at full speed. His car was faster than our van, and pretty soon he caught up with us.

We all started screaming as we saw what was in his hand! An ax!

He began driving wildly with one hand, and shaking the axe at us with the other. He was not a happy camper, as they say.

He continued to follow us as he drove down the road. I didn't know a pick ax for digging holes was a good weapon to solve people's relationships.

We finally lost him as we drove onto the highway.

YOU DON'T HAVE TO LIVE LIKE A WILD MAN

With some people, you never know why they are so angry. Maybe they have stored up anger from past incidents. Or they might have just decided, that you are the person they are going to dump all their frustrations from their past 15 years!

In fact, it would have been better if the extremist had taken a break with us, and came on the picnic. Built up stress will cause even more problems.

You don't have to live like a wild man, waving a pickaxe and threatening the lives of others around you!

Take a break. Be good to yourself.

Recognize your needs and take care of them.

Even Jesus told his disciples to come aside, and rest, after they ministered to people.

TAKING A BREAK DOES WONDERS

After creating the world, God Himself rested on the seventh day. If God takes a break, you can too! Don't forget to take time off. Get refreshed, and look after yourself.

Many people's favorite part of the Bible is Psalm 23. It says, "The Lord is my Shepherd. He makes me lie down in green pastures and leads me beside still waters."

You may have many hurdles before you. But even mountain climbers rest before finally climbing to the summit. In order to make the last steep ascent, they need to be in top physical emotional condition.

The Bible tells us to love our neighbor as ourself. We always focus on the first part, but forget the second part.

So love yourself! Do nice things for yourself.

Be kind to yourself.

DON'T REFUSE THE GOOD THINGS

One year, we won a holiday at a gold crown resort on the Mediterranean Turkish seacoast. The pictures showed white beaches, swimming pool, the waterslide, and even a hotel petting zoo complete with ponies for the kids.

The holiday was completely free and all-inclusive. The only thing required was to go to an office, and pick up the vouchers. We didn't have to do anything else!

All we had to do was show up. That was the one condition.

We could have refused the offer, and told the people that we didn't deserve it. We could have told them we were too busy helping other people.

Don't refuse the good things that come your way. Don't think that you are made of steel. Recognize the fact that you need a break. Take a break, or you might be the one that gets broken.

We enjoyed our time at that resort! Eating ice cream everyday, relaxing by the sea, sand between our toes. It was so enjoyable. It was a long drive to get to the hotel. But it was worth every mile!

You could say, "It's not worth the trip. I have so much work to do anyways. And I hate packing."

What's worse is not taking the trip! Practicality doesn't always rule in life. Work hard to enjoy life! The effort it takes to love yourself is worth it. Otherwise, you will just keep going and going and going.

The Energizer bunny advertisement is good for sales, but not the whole story. You are a person. You can't just keep going and going. You are not the Energizer bunny!

You forget how valuable you are!

Take the effort; take the time to love yourself. This principle will help you get further along in your life than you can imagine.

The Bible says, "Taste and see that God is good." If you don't taste and see, if you don't accept the free vacation offer, you will not realize what a beautiful world the Lord has created!

Just because the hotel is free, it does not guarantee that you will enjoy your stay. Learn to relax! Resting is being satisfied with yourself. You realize that you have a long race to run. That race is of utmost importance. So take a break and be refreshed!

Sometimes loving yourself is something you've never learned. You might need to take extra lessons on that subject! So hang out with people, friends, and family and learn from them. Find someone who knows how to enjoy life and tag along. You'll never regret those extra lessons.

SWITZERLAND, HERE WE COME

It had been the dream of my precious wife Mary Jane to see the Swiss Alps. One summer while we were in Germany for training, that very opportunity arose. A friend graciously allowed us to use their car for about 2 weeks to go see Switzerland.

Mary Jane was ecstatic! The scenery was absolutely magnificent. We drove along winding mountain roads, drove through long underground tunnels, and just gazed at the mountains.

Switzerland was a beautiful place indeed. When we went, all we had was enough food and gas money to drive there and back.

How can we enjoy a holiday in Switzerland without any extra pocket money for treats and extras? We thought.

We consoled ourselves with the thought that we'd at least be able to see the sights.

Mary Jane had a friend in Switzerland that she hadn't seen for years. So we stopped in to see her and her husband. We had a great time visiting and talking. As we left their apartment, she said, "Wait! I have something for you!"

As she handed us an envelope full of cash, we just stared at it.

We were so excited about that envelope. Now, we had lots of extra money. The very next day, we went out and bought some of the best ice cream I had ever tasted. We treated ourselves to many bars of chocolate, as we enjoyed the scenery of the Swiss countryside.

We stopped in little Swiss chalets for fondue, wandered around the shops looking at souvenirs. On the way back, after being refreshed, we stopped in to see some other friends of ours.

"Ian! Mary Jane! You guys look so happy! What happened?" they said with wonder.

Mary Jane and I both knew it was because we were treated and pampered during our time in Switzerland. The "extra" had been so important!

CREATIVITY AND IDEAS WILL COME TO YOU

Your success in your life is also dependent on your being refreshed, renewed, and rejuvenated.

An inventor we met recently told how most of his inventions and solutions have come to him while he has been sleeping. His group of scientists testifies to the same thing. Take time to ensure you are operating at the top of your game. That way, creativity and ideas will come to you.

If these inventors had not been taking time to take care of themselves, they would not have found solutions to incredibly complex problems. Their very solutions have impacted many people.

To refuse to take a break is a denial of the frailty of the human frame. You are a unique person with many unique gifts and talents.

But those gifts and talents will not come out if you are tired.

Some people take time by walking in nature. Others take time for themselves by shopping or exercising. Movies and books that celebrate life will inspire and motivate you. People are rejuvenated in many different ways. There are no stereotypes.

Celebrate your life. Have mercy on yourself and those around you by taking time to ensure that you are all happy and rested.

DISNEYLAND: THE GREAT ESCAPE

After being put on the WANTED list, daily life became very stressful for me. We had lots of phone calls, inquiries.

Information was being leaked to the police and the media. We even had an undercover reporter who kept asking for a job at our Alo Dua Prayer Hotlines. Some of our friends wanted to help us.

They sent us to Disneyland, providing passes and also lodging! My family and I enjoyed Disneyland every single day. The Turkish police had no clue where we were. It turned out to be the perfect way to let things cool down in Turkey for me!

It was quite an experience. In Turkey, Joy and Josh were used to a life of precaution because I had been arrested so many times. They were used to looking over their shoulder to make sure we were not being followed. Disneyland was a whole new world for them.

Everyday, we ate ice cream and watched the parade.

RELAX AND LET LOOSE

Joshua was enthralled by the rides, the technology, and the shows. In Turkey, young as he was, Joshua would often act as my security together with our staff. He could spot police coming a mile away. He especially enjoyed not having to watch every moment now.

The train engineer got on the loudspeaker and announced, "We have a special guest today - Princess Joy is here with us!"

The whole trainload of guests applauded. Joy laughed. I was so happy to see her laugh and enjoy all the attention.

My wife Mary Jane cried when she heard about the gift of a Disneyland trip. She needed a break from all the security issues.

Our family was so stressed out. But slowly, we had to learn to relax and let loose.

THE LAND WHERE DREAMS COME TRUE

Disneyland advertises that it is the land where dreams come true. The park is full of rides, cartoon characters, junk food, and all types of amusing activities! People plan for months on end, dreaming of their vacation in Disneyland.

But once they get there, many people can it a challenge.

People pay a lot of money to travel to Disneyland. But you can't force anyone to have a good time.

Give yourself permission to relax, laugh, and just have fun. Give yourself permission to enjoy life.

Just as Disneyland is full of myths and stories to entertain families, many parents have their own myths that they propagate about Disneyland as well!

One myth is about the parade. There is a daily parade on the main street of Disneyland. It's very strange, but you'll see many of the parents sitting on the sidewalk for up to two hours before the parade starts.

They tell their kids that they need to get there early in order get a good seat on the sidewalk to be able to see the parade.

But the truth is that the parents are just tired. And this is the time that parents take a break.

People sometimes find that having fun can become a chore too. So take a break! Have some fun!

TAKE THE PLUNGE

Virtually all workplaces require their staff to take an annual vacation. Why? This is for the sake of the staff and for the sake of the company. Every manager knows that he needs ready workers. Refreshed workers will be more productive in the long run.

In order to be in the cutting edge in business, the company will ensure that you take your vacation time.

Take the plunge! You don't have to be so serious. Watch your efficiency go to a higher level when you are rested. Creativity is a must for problem-solving and business ventures!

Many accidents happen because of being overstressed. Your body can only take so much. If you don't take it easy, you increase your chances of getting hurt. And then the occupational therapist will come looking for you!

Whenever someone hurts himself, they have to go through therapy to get back the full range motion of the injured body part. And in many instances, this can become a very long process.

Why not love yourself and allow yourself to be rejuvenated? You are one very special person. There is no one like you. We need you to be up and running!

You are significant and important. You are an amazing person with important things to do. So take time to be renewed, and continue to run your race with vigor.

VISIT THE TURKISH BATH

Exhausted, not sure how we could go anymore – the three of us men were so tired! We had been traveling for days. The police had arrested us on that trip, and then let us go after a while.

I kept falling asleep at the wheel and scaring my two friends who were trying to sleep in the back seat. It was starting to get dark when we came to a village in the middle of nowhere.

Lo and behold! There is a Turkish bath! We stopped, because we were in such need of a rest. It proved to be a good decision. The Turkish bath was so hot. The hot towels and the steam were exactly what we needed!

And as we three men rested on the hot slabs of marble, I began to feel like a new person. After our time there, we were ready to go again.

When you are tired, lonely, and at the end of your rope - it's time for you to have something new! You need a treat.

You need to be pampered and renewed. Right at this moment,

recognize your need.

Your break is ready! The appointment with the spa has been made for you! The paid vacation starts now.

Your potential will not be fully realized without the necessary and needed refreshment. So sit back and relax. Receive and rest.

DR. IAN HERINGA

CHAPTER 13

WHAT DO YOU NEED TO SUCCEED

When we first arrived in Turkey – getting a long-term visa was paramount. This was a constant struggle. And we were quite concerned about it too.

A friend named Gordon in Canada connected us with his close friend in Turkey. This man was a high-ranking government official.

Walking into this government official's office – I was shocked! His office was at least half as big as your house, if not as big as your whole house.

I spent time in his office getting to know him and talk English together. I'd come in to see him and while waiting in his lobby, people would stream past me with gifts for him (this was a much more efficient and faster way of getting their projects done).

Whenever he'd pull out a cigarette, 3 guys would scramble for a lighter. Now that is something!

When it came time for me to get my visa, this government official got the lawyer from his office, a translator, and another staff member to escort us to the police station.

His driver drove us in a government car. He parked right in front of the main entrance. It is illegal to do that. But you see, you can park anywhere if you have a government car.

The lawyer and the translator, as well as the official's assistant walked in front of me, bypassing the visa offices. They walked straight into the office of the police chief.

We sat down, drank some tea. And papers were filed. The lawyer worked on them over the next few months.

Everything was done without my lifting a finger.

I did not have to pay for anything except for the visa. I didn't have to navigate my way through the different offices on my own.

EVERYTHING IS PREPARED FOR YOU

Your way is prepared ahead of you. You might say you don't know how it's ever going to work out.

You might feel like nothing will ever change. But many times, you will find that God has already prepared everything for you. He already has people in the right places at the right time for your miracle.

God is guiding your steps. He works out your schedule. Things will get working and going, so that you are not hindered.

The government official risked his name for my sake. He was my backing. The car driver knew where to go. The lawyer knew what applications had to be processed. He knew how to fill out the application, and answer the questions.

Thankfully, the translator helped me so much, so I could talk with the lawyer, the car driver, and even the police chief. The resources and personnel are ready. The way and the procedure have already been worked out.

When the government official was my backing, no questions

were asked. All he had to do was snap his fingers and my work got done. For him, it was only a question of which fingers to snap.

You don't need to know everything. Just allow yourself to be helped. Allow God to back you up.

WHEN THE EARTH SHAKES

The whole team talked excitedly, as our van bumped down the road. We were on our way to the city of Haci Bektas in Eastern Turkey.

We had been invited to attend an Alevi festival. Alevis are a separate sect of Islam. They don't go to a regular mosque. They have music in their meetings, plus a lot of dancing. The Alevi elders run the meetings.

Upon our arrival in the town of Nevsehir, we headed to city hall and confirmed our registration. The city was decorated with banners, children ran laughing and shouting on the streets, as their parents listened to Alevi leaders, politicians, and singers on the big stage.

We registered to have a stand at the fair. Looking forward to meeting all kinds of new people, we opened up with our display of books.

People crowded around, trying to see what why our bookstand was attracting so many people. There was lots of interest, and thousands of people received a copy of the New Testament. We made many friends.

It was a busy week. The weather was hot and dusty. But we were having a great time. The stand across from us was a communist group. They were not happy with the attention that our New Testament bookstand was getting. The Communists complained to the police.

The police arrived, walked up to our stand, and said, "You are under arrest!"

Five of us on the team were arrested. One of our guys, Ufuk, had gone for a coffee break. I was so glad that at least Ufuk had been able to escape arrest.

They confiscated all our books and all our personal belongings.

We had to give a statement about what we were doing in Haci Bektas. Then, we were taken to a doctor who gave us a medical exam. This is to show that the police did not beat us in any way.

The whole process was very intimidating. I didn't know what would happen next.

As we sat in the waiting room of the doctor's office, a news flash appeared on the screen.

The words "Attention: A 7.2 Earthquake has happened near Istanbul," scrolled across the screen.

Istanbul? Not Istanbul? My wife and kids are in Istanbul! I thought.

"Sir, sir! I have to make a phone call. I need to find out if my family is okay."

"Sorry Ian. Prisoners are not allowed to use the telephone here," the guard replied.

I sat down on the bench, feeling very worried.

A 7.2 earthquake is very bad. Very bad indeed. Protect Mary Jane. Protect Joy. Protect Josh. Protect the rest of our staff. Help me to contact them. Please help me to get out of here.

IN UNCERTAIN TIMES - BELIEVE

My friends and I had no idea what would happen next. They took us back to the police station.

"Please, I need to reach my family. Please let me make a call. Just one call. Please..." I pleaded with the police. My request fell on deaf ears. I was flatly refused.

"I am a Canadian citizen. I should be allowed a phone call. I was not even allowed to call my lawyer. Here! I have part of the Turkish Constitution in my wallet. It says here that there is religious freedom in Turkey. You cannot arrest me just for being a Christian." I shouted.

No one took any notice. One policeman looked up and said, "You! Sit!" So we waited. And waited. And waited. The hours dragged on, and my thoughts ran wild.

Mary Jane... Joy... Joshua... I have to get back to them. I have to find out if they are okay. Mary Jane... Joy... Joshua... God, hear me! Hear my prayer! Protect everyone of my family and staff. Anguish filled my heart.

A tall young police officer came swaggering in the room.
"You will soon be informed of your fate," he said with a sneer.

A FREE RIDE OUT OF TURKEY

Half an hour later, we learned that the police were going to deport us. That means we were about to get a free ride out of Turkey.

All five of us on the team were piled into a police van. Two police were ordered to drive us to the main city in the province.

We tried to keep our spirits up and encouraged, as we bumped along the road in the old police van. The van stalled several times on the trip. I kept looking for a chance to make a run for it. But there was none. Not even a window of a couple seconds.

They are sending us out of the country. But I have to get back to Istanbul. I need to find out if my wife and kids are okay. I can't be deported out of the country now like a criminal. I'm no criminal. We don't even know what the charges are. I have to get out of this van! Now!

All along, Ufuk who escaped arrest had followed us. He took the keys to our van, and inconspicuously followed us from police station, to the doctor, back to the police station, and on to the next city. The police never detected him.

As soon as Ufuk found out what happened, he called Mary Jane. He had to try around 10 times before he got through. Mary Jane and the kids survived the earthquake okay. The rest of the staff was okay as well. The walls of our home had cracks. Vases and bookshelves had crashed, but thankfully, everyone was okay, despite being rather traumatized.

Mary Jane immediately called the Canadian embassy.

"IT'S FOR YOU, IT'S YOUR WIFE"

We were sitting in the police station's office as they were processing our papers to deport us. All of a sudden, the phone rang!

The policeman picked up the phone, and his eyes grew wide!

"It's for you. It's your wife. How on earth did she find you?

How did she find out we brought you here?" The incredulous look on his face was scrapbook-worthy.

"Oh honey! Are you okay? I've been so worried about you and the kids." Mary Jane and I talked quickly. I told her the situation and how we were about to be deported out of Turkey.

As soon as I finished talking with Mary Jane, the phone rang again.

"It's your Canadian embassy." they said.

Those two phone calls turned everything around for us. The embassy assured us that we would not be deported. Hours later, we were free!

DEMONSTRATED LOVE TO YOU

No one can stand in your way when God is for you. Not at all! It says in the Scriptures that, "He demonstrates his goodness to you - so much so that your enemies are put to shame."

That means God is ready and willing to pour out so much goodness on you. Today it is good. Tomorrow it is good. God never changes. His character or opinion of you never changes. And the amount that God is willing to be good to you never changes.

Hang on! Because God is about to demonstrate His feelings for you! Take a test drive. Let the demonstration begin. This compassion and provision will open doors. Expect the expanded office space. Expect the mortgage to get paid off. Expect your children to graduate with honors.

When the blessing comes, it brings no sorrow with it. This means no bad stuff mixed in. Keep a humble heart. And keep looking up. Love for you is about to be demonstrated.

SELLING LIKE HOTCAKES

We had a full day ahead of us. Kevin and I loaded up the car with copies of God's book of love. Kevin was new on the job and eager to learn.

Jim came along with his video camera to record stories about how people's lives were being changed by God's book of love. He was going to make a great documentary.

Kevin and I spent the whole day meeting people, and making deliveries all over the city. Jim was getting lots of good footage. Finally, we came to our last stop - our biggest group of distributors.

The orange bookseller stands in Ankara would sell out of Turkish New Testaments every single time. We tried to constantly keep them in stock, but those New Testaments were selling like hotcakes!

ERASE THE TAPE, QUICK!

Pulling up to the sidewalk, I parked right there on the busy street. Kevin and I started with the deliveries. Storeowners would bring a trolley and load the New Testaments and bring boxes back to their bookstand.

Jim positioned himself to shoot from the corner. He filmed us coming back and forth to the different storeowners with their trolleys.

And while waiting for storeowners to come out to the car and pick up their orders of books, Jim would work on his grocery list.

A local bank guard began to get very suspicious. He watched Jim work with his camera, and then make notes on a list. Jim would go back to the camera, and then work on his list again.

The bank guard became alarmed. What was that American cameraman filming and writing down?

The bank guard called the police. So when Kevin and I came back to the car, we walked straight into the police. They had been waiting for us.

The police had already taken Jim and shoved him in the back of the police car. I could see him nervously sitting there, wistfully looking out of the police car window.

I made a signal to him, *"the footage, the footage..."*

Jim looked at me with a strange look, and then understood. He gave me a thumbs-up from inside the police car, and unobtrusively, put the camera under his coat. With a swift motion, he put his finger on the "erase" button and held it there.

The policeman began to grill Kevin in fluent English about our activities. Kevin and I tried to stall so that Jim would have enough time to erase all his footage from that day.

"What are you foreigners doing here?" the policeman asked in perfect English. He continued to ask more questions in English

OFISIKLES: THE BOMBSHELL QUESTION

But then he hit us with a bombshell question, "What are the ofisikles?"

"Ofisikles?" Kevin asked.

"Yes, ofisikles. You know ofisikles?" The officer asked.

"I'm sorry, sir. I don't know what an 'ofisikle' is," Kevin ventured.

We looked at each other, wondering what the policeman meant. For half an hour, he kept repeating and asking Kevin what were the "ofisikles". Whenever the policeman would ask Kevin about the "ofisikles", Kevin would say plainly and truthfully,

"I do not know what an ofisikle is!"

We tried our best not to laugh, and keep a straight face. The policeman had done very well in learning English; he was very fluent - except for the word "ofisikle".

WHAT'S ON YOUR GROCERY LIST?

By this time, Jim had been able to erase all the footage, for which we were very relieved.

There on the sidewalk, we waited until a high-ranking police officer came. The high-ranking officer questioned us some more.

"Sir, I wasn't taking notes. I was working on my grocery list," Jim showed his grocery list to the police. After inspecting the list very closely, and finding no footage on the camera — the police had no choice but to let us go.

I made it home just in time for supper. My wife and kids had been so worried because I should've been back a long time ago.

But when I told them over our supper of fried chicken and

mashed potatoes about what had happened to Jim, Kevin and I - my kids just giggled the whole dinnertime.

After dessert, my kids went around the house singing, "Ofisikles, ofisikles, oh, oh, ofisikles!" Yes. That 'ofisikle' phrase gave Jim just enough time to erase everything on the tape! And to this day, nobody still knows what an "ofisikle" is!

STRESS CAN BE FUN, WELL SOMETIMES…

There are times when the pressure is on! And there doesn't seem to be a solution.

Make out your wants list. Write out your concerns. Take note of your needs. Ask for help, because we are needy people. We all need somebody pulling for us.

This is a fact. He loves to hear your little prayers, and your big needs. What about the medium-sized and oversized prayers? God loves to hear from you.

He loves it when you relate to him on a daily basis. Even when we get angry, He sees through the anger to our need. He doesn't justify our anger. But in His compassion, He sees the need and understands.

Don't you love to spoil your son or daughter at Christmas? Don't you love the look of excitement and surprise as they open their presents?

People who are encouraged and strengthened can be more productive. Studies have shown that a positive working atmosphere brings more results.

JUSTICE IS ON ITS WAY

To lack is to be human. When we think we don't lack, when we are not needy, perhaps pride has began to set in. God always has more in store for you.

Your lack can be turned into your miracle. This can be the very opportunity to allow God to demonstrate His love to you. God is not as distant as you think. Just let Him know that you need more finances. Tell him about your needs for time, personnel, space, resources, knowledge, and wisdom.

"God is not unjust; he will not forget your work and the love you have shown him as you have helped his people and continue to help them. We want each of you to show this same diligence to the very end, in order to make your hope sure," Hebrews 6:10-11 (NIV).

Why did this disaster happen? Why do horrible events unfold? How about looking at it the other way?

We live in a broken world, but because of God's love for us – our lives can be healed. The very disaster or crisis that would have otherwise swallowed you up, can be used to promote you to the top!

CHAPTER 14

I RECEIVE

He just broke down. Right there on the phone.

"Ian, I just don't know what to do. I'm at my wit's end. I have so many debts that I can't take it anymore. Would it be a sin to kill myself?"

I was talking to a guy named Ugur. He had called our Help Hotlines, and then had come to church several times.

"I'm in despair. I can't pay my debtors," Ugur sobbed.

"It says that he who is forgiven much, loves much…." I began to tell the following story.

To illustrate the principle of forgiveness, Jesus told a story. One man owed a huge amount of money to his boss. The man went to his boss and begged for mercy. The boss forgave the debt and totally wiped out the man's payment plan.

But on the way out, the man found a guy who owed him a little bit of money. He began to choke the guy, and screamed for his money back. The man wouldn't show mercy at all, even if it were just a small amount.

"Ugur, do you understand? You can be forgiven your debts. Just start out by forgiving others. Forgive yourself. Receive the fact that you are forgiven and receive God's grace, God's miracles, and a new lease on life."

FLASH: FORGIVENESS AFFECTS FINANCES

I didn't hear anything else from Ugur for about 6 months. But one day, right out of the blue, he called me.

"Ian, I'm coming to church tomorrow. You'll never believe it. I paid all my debts. And to top it all off - I'm coming in a brand new car!"

He arrived at church the next day, all excited! He told us all about what had happened.

Ugur had a lot of bitterness and hardness stored up in his heart. He was angry with his parents, especially with his father, and he was bitter against his family's business partners who had embezzled their money.

FORGIVE OTHERS, FORGIVE SELF

One by one, he spent a lot of time forgiving each person and each offense as he remembered them.

Ugur explained to us how his desire to live slowly returned. The burden didn't seem so heavy. His passion for his business and his family returned anew.

He realized that the only way to move ahead was to keep on receiving the fact that he was forgiven.

Ugur explained that as he understood being forgiven, his business started to pick up again. He felt that his bitterness towards life, family, and others had choked his desire to live and succeed.

Ugur poured out his heart, asking God to forgive him for his pride and selfishness. He asked forgiveness for his envy and jealousy. He instead felt that he had been given a new lease on life. Ugur couldn't explain everything. But he knew that conquering his financial debts was somehow linked to his being forgiven. The more he forgave himself and others, his financial debts lessened.

Parked in the parking lot outside the church was his new car. This, for him, was a symbol of his new lease on life. He was filled with a new hope.

FREELY RECEIVE

As you read this page, you may feel that you have been singled out for hardship. You may feel that life has not treated you well. Even if it seems that no one has shown kindness to you – don't despair.

You are not being singled out. You are getting ready to receive.

Jesus told his disciples, "Freely you have received, so freely give." (Matthew 10:8). Freely receive God's compassion on you. Freely receive the love that you need. You are to give away what you receive. But until you have received it – you have nothing to give.

Freely forgive yourself. Those past mistakes cannot hold you back. All the bitterness and hardness against yourself is holding you captive to the same cycles.

With one hand, hold on to love and receive forgiveness. Psalm 91:4 says, "He will cover you with his feathers, and under his wings you will find refuge; his faithfulness will be your shield and rampart."

Receive God's cleansing rain over you. It's time to be washed, and renewed, and start again on a whole new level. Perhaps you were never taught to forgive, to apologize, or to make wrongs right. But now you know. So start practicing with yourself.

Receive grace. And as you work through different situations, receive "well done". Accept the thumbs up and big smile. God is not amazed at your mistakes. He's not horrified about your mess.

You have been called out. You have been chosen to win! And

now is the time for you to run your race with fresh vigor.

Your time to receive is today. Sit back and see all that has been done in your life. Accept all that He wants to do for you for your future. Receive a new fresh start from the Lord. Today, He is removing your yoke of hardness and bitterness, envy and jealousy, and turning the clock back. Just ask Him!

As I write this with tears, knowing that you need this, I'm confident in you that your heart is open to receive.

Now on the other hand, you can start releasing those family, friends, neighbors, and business partners who owe you, burned you, and swindled you. You can start on your new journey of forgiveness.

THE BEST OF MY LIFE

The first time I saw Mary Jane, I couldn't help but wonder who she was. She had a smile that resembled the sun, and she was dressed so beautifully.

A beautiful Filipina that carried herself with impeccable style, I kept my eye out for Mary Jane at different places around the church. She was a high school teacher. And because Mary Jane's mother passed away within weeks of their arrival from the Philippines, she was also a busy stand-in for the rest of her family.

Mary Jane and I had very similar interests, which was fortunate. And many times, she would come with me as I drove the Sunday School bus to pick up kids who needed a ride to church.

Mary Jane was busy. In fact, she was extremely busy with her job and family, and very hard to get. Or maybe she was playing hard to get as well. But when we both joined a team to go to South America to build a school for children, our friendship grew much closer.

In fact, I decided to appoint myself as Mary Jane's official bodyguard. Where we were working in Bogota definitely wasn't safe. And once again, I found in Mary Jane a wonderful friend. She returned the favor by translating for me into Spanish as I preached.

The more time I spent with Mary Jane, the more I knew I found that I was falling head over heels in love. Mary Jane abounds in beauty, and I knew she was the right woman for me. She had the same passion to help people and go to other nations. Mary Jane called me her "spiritual man". And I wrote her a poem or letter every single day.

Finally, I popped the question and she agreed to marry me. We lived in a small trailer, as we both studied at Prairie Bible Institute to prepare to go into the ministry.

Together, we learned to get by with very little. But it was one of the best times of our lives.

YOU ARE A BREAKTHROUGH PERSON

No matter whether you are divorced, have an incredible marriage, or if you are hoping to get married, or determinedly single – you are precious in God's sight.

He is directing your steps, and has a bountiful life in store for you.

And when you need healing from brokenness, you can become an overcomer. You have not given up.

Take out that big eraser that removes every stain of condemnation.

"Come now, let us reason together," says the Lord. "Though your sins are like scarlet, they shall be as white as snow; though they are red as crimson, they shall be like wool." Isaiah 1:18 (NIV)

You are a new beginner, a fresh starter.

God's heart is exploding with compassion, healing, and expectation. And it's all for you!

YOU CAN

You have been faithful, a survivor, overcomer, and now is the time for you to fly. No more punishing yourself, no more putting yourself down.

You are a breakthrough person. God has prepared so many good things for you - which have been stored up. Now, they are being released to you. God has high hopes for you.

And He also gives the strength and courage to walk in those

steps. You have great potential.

You can.

YOU ARE HONORABLE

When I went into the nation of Iraq, the very air was tense. Because of the war, people were afraid and scared. I tried to learn some of the language. I wanted to be able to say "hello" and "thank you", as well as a good phrase to introduce myself.

I decided that the proper phrase to use to introduce myself would be something like, "Here is a gift for you." I wanted to be able to give aid, and God's message of love to each family living in a tent.

I learned a phrase, and repeated it over and over. But a strange thing happened. As other team members and I went to each tent, saying my little phrase in the Iraqi language, each time a man would stand up, look very proud, throw his shoulders back, and step forward to receive my package.

I didn't understand this phenomenon. Each tent was so incredibly hospitable and gracious. Each man that stood up would offer to show me around the camp. I was able to meet many families. We made a lot of friends.

Some days later, I realized the sentence that I was saying to each tent was not, "Here is a gift for you."

Instead, I was saying, "Who's the head man here?" And of course this was the perfect sentence!

Honor is an important part of the Middle Eastern culture. And as I honored people, they wanted to receive.

I PICK YOU

Today, God is walking into your tent. He says, "I pick you!"

You are so special, lovable, incredible, unique, and treasured.

You are exceptional. The person who you really are is not always seen. Deep down inside, that is the true you.

"How precious to me are your thoughts, O God! How vast is the sum of them. Were I to count them, they would outnumber the grains of sand. When I awake, I am still with you." (Psalm 139:17,18 NIV).

You have great promise, but you also may have been wounded in the process of living life. You want to change. This also means you are teachable.

So live like you are loved perfectly!

Perfect love is what brings the best out of you. Perfect love is not colored by your history.

Perfect love is not colored by anything at all.

THEY GOT THE WRONG GUY!

The day after we were featured on the national news for three nights in a row, a mob gathered at the door of our church building.

About 70 men were shouting and chanting slogans. They had flags and sticks. The mob tore the church sign down, and tried to break open the door.

Our landlord came to see what was happening. Within minutes, the mob started beating him up.

Later he told me, "Ian, if I had known... if I had only known, I would have packed my gun. You know I always carry my gun everywhere I go. I can't believe I was so foolish."

That same day, our daughter Joy was on her way to the church with her friend. Joy saw the mob, stopped in her tracks, and they discreetly blended in with the onlookers.

As they walked past, Joy quietly asked one of the bystanders what was happening.

TAKE THE TAXI CAB

"Big brother, what is happening?" she inquired.

"Oh! You know that the church was on TV last night? Well, the mob beat up the landlord."

Our landlord was punched, and had a black eye.

Five police cars arrived on the scene, lights flashing, and with loudspeakers blaring. Shouting commands, the police officers quickly dispersed the mob, before it became bigger. They started to investigate the mob scene.

Joy tried to quickly get out of there. Some of the men in the mob recognized Joy from the church service on TV.

They began to notice Joy and her friend. They walked faster. The men started shouting.

Just as Joy was about to break out into a run, she spotted a yellow taxi and they got in! Safe!

EASY VS. HARD

God has a solution already on its way for you! We often tend to be hard on ourselves or make our lives harder than it needs to be. So jump in the taxi! Make life easy for yourself.

Sometimes we resist the word "easy". But when God says something is easy, then it is easy. Look and see if there are ways in your home, office, and school where you can make things easier for yourself.

Take those steps to change your life. Get in the taxi instead of just trying to run away on foot.

"What is the price of two sparrows – one copper coin? But not a single sparrow can fall to the ground without your Father knowing it." (Matthew 10:29 NLT).

In a time of crisis you could be stubbornly walking, when you should be riding. Your cab to your future is here. It's time to really experience and see that God is good!

DR. IAN HERINGA

CHAPTER 15

APPRECIATE YOUR OWN TALENTS

My family and children were back in our coal-heated apartment trying to stay warm. The heat would only come on twice a day. And the water cuts in the city were making life very difficult. After 5 days, we still didn't have water. Ewww! Life was hard... But...

I was struggling. I started going to language classes at the Turkish University. At 29 years of age, I was the oldest student in the class.

The teacher would grill me every Monday about what I had done on the weekend. I always dreaded Monday mornings, because I would have to tell a story in Turkish about what I did on the weekend. That seemed to be the instructor's favorite question.

One time he grilled me so much, I thought the buttons were

going to pop off my shirt, because of the pressure.

I would dream about just playing hookey. Yes sir, when you can't beat them – don't join them. Hide, flee, escape, and do whatever you can – but just make it look good, I would joke.

Wow! There has to be an easier way to learn this language! I thought.

I was supposed to learn the language. I was supposed to be able to talk, and communicate with people in this foreign country.

I would learn a few short phrases and practice them daily. And it was hard. Verbs, nouns, adjectives – I couldn't understand why they were all in the same sentence. So there's hope for you and me.

Learning the language took me some years, before I could speak well. I finally came to grips with the fact that I needed to readjust my expectations.

I had to focus on the things I was good at. It's times like this when you don't have to be so hard on yourself.

YOUR PURPOSE AND DESTINY WILL FIND YOU

There are always other things you can do, instead of being the "ideal" you that everybody including your parents, relatives, neighbors, and peers say you should be. It's time to scramble, and pick up the pieces. So let's get busy!

My next role in getting out among the people was riskier, than I had ever imagined. My next role was to be my purpose and destiny.

Find yourself right where you are supposed to be. In the middle of doing what looks like everyday things, find your destiny.

You might not realize it, but in the middle of so many difficulties and struggles, you are about to get really good at doing this one thing.

There can be a few hurdles, mistakes, doubts, and money concerns – but this new dream is really you. But when you do what God has for you, you will realize that this is who you are. And that you are doing what you are meant to do!

Your purpose and destiny will find you.

Don't be so down on yourself. Give yourself a little leeway, a break or two, and you'll see that things will start to shine. You will shine soon, I promise you.

It's easier than you think. What you love to do is your destiny. It may not look that professional, or polished to others, to your father, mother, or friends, but hey! It's really you. So let's come to terms with that, so you can keep reading.

A dream grew in my heart to give out the book that gave me hope and purpose. I wanted to make the book, that had so dramatically altered my outlook on life, available to anyone who wanted it in Turkey.

PAYDAY IS COMING

As I focused on my dream, the impossible also happened as a side result. I began preaching in Turkish!

Everywhere I go in Turkey, people ask me how I learned Turkish. I just smile and say, "Just keep doing what you are good at, the Turkish will come."

Whether you are running, or walking, you are still winning. You are increasing in skill and in accuracy. You are improving, and getting to the top of your game. You are learning secrets of how to do your own destiny that no one else has discovered.

Soon you will be able to make it, because of your relentlessness. You've kept plodding on, running even when you're tired, with too many things on your plate. It's going to get better. Life will improve.

To put it simply, you are giving of yourself to become better. This new you is really likable and proficient. The secrets you are learning now are the things that will carry you, propel you. Others will want to know how you made it.

It's time for the rain of abundance to come on your life. The dedication and passion is paying off.

Payday is coming. It may seem impossible to you. But to God, it's not.

Sometimes the critics can make it difficult, but that's exactly what's keeping you on track. The pressure and hard work is changing you, and making you blossom.

Because of your immense potential, one of the tools to get you fully sharpened is pressure. Critics, lack of finances, and struggles with bad habits all fit into this category.

The critics don't realize what they're doing to you and me. Actually, it's the other way around. It's you and I who don't realize how the critics are helping. They are the detox that keeps our hearts and motives focused and pure.

You see, you are not just pure muscle, potential, beauty, and cleverness.

Yes, you are handsome, talented, and hard working, but you have a bunch of stuff that only detox and detox alone can get rid of. So, hang in there. You are going through detox!

THE UNIQUE ANGLE

STAR Newspaper wrote, "This is the best example of missionary work in the country, because they give out New Testaments under police supervision. There is no crime in what they are doing."

In the year 2000, we gave out a total of 65,000 New Testaments. Thousands of people phoned in to the Alo Dua Help Hotlines, and 18,000 requests came in from all over the country.

Aksiyon Magazine says, "Alo Dua [Ministry] gets the highest ratings in the media." Over one thousand national newspaper articles have been written about our ministry work. TEMPO magazine: "Protestant Pastor Gives Miracles to Muslims."

Zaman Newspaper, "No one is saying 'stop' to them! They [Alo Dua] are gripping Turkey like an octopus. And with all speed, continue their activities. Like a big fan to every corner of this land, these missionaries are running like horses, and are using newspaper advertisements to gain followers. They are giving out New Testaments."

Aksam Newspaper, "On the streets of Istanbul, they are giving out New Testaments!"

Star Newspaper, "The missionaries are hard at work giving out New Testaments."

Zaman Newspaper, "The people who are giving out New Testaments have been very active. In reaction to this, Korans are being distributed for free."

Gozcu Newspaper, "Alo Dua Hotlines have been opened! In the one of the busiest areas of Istanbul, they are giving out New

Testaments!'

Aktuel Newspaper, "Prayer can now be requested over the internet. They prayed, and he found work!"

TURNED INTO KINDNESS

My associate and I went into the registry. I had some paperwork to get done. There were 20 people ahead of us. One guy told us he had already been waiting for an hour.

We asked the secretary, "Is there a way we could get our work done faster? We're really in a hurry."

As I appealed to the secretary, I noticed the manager of the registry pointing his webcam at us. First he focused the webcam at me, then at my associate, and then back at me.

I turned to the secretary who was saying, "I'm sorry sir. There's nothing that can be done. You just have to wait. We only have a few staff working today, you might have to wait around 2 hours."

We sat down and tried to make ourselves comfortable. This was going to be a long two hours!

But then I saw the manager motioning to us to come into his office. He had seen us on the TV news.

"I was just video chatting to my brother. He lives in another city. I told him, 'Guess who I have in my office?' When my brother saw you through the webcam, he recognized you from the TV news too."

I was so surprised. So that's why he was pointing the webcam at my associate and me.

"What brings you to our registry? Is there anything I can do to help?" he asked kindly.

I explained our predicament, and the urgency to get our paperwork done. The manager took our paperwork, and did it right then and there himself.

He was happy to help us - his new friends. And we were glad to have our work done quicker than we imagined. Within 15 minutes, I was walking out of that office!

POST OFFICE FAVOR

We pushed past the crowds of people waiting in line at the post office to pay their bills. My friend got the letters from our post office box, and I mailed some letters that had to go out.

The manager of the post office waved me down. "Ian! Ian! I saw you on TV."

He shared how his wife was an insomniac. She would only get a few hours of sleep each night. This brought on a lot of stress on him as well.

"If she doesn't sleep, I don't sleep," he complained. "And of course the medicine she is taking is not helping at all. The side effects are worse than the problem."

He ushered us into his office, and asked if we could pray for his wife.

The tough post office manager began to cry. Right there in his office, we asked God for help to be given to this precious family.

Sometimes, we don't understand the stresses people are going through. But when we stop and help, we can bring about change in their lives.

UNDERSTANDING STRESS

The post office manager was a busy man. The building was full of people. The line-up of people waiting to pay bills was backed up, almost up to the door.

But the post office manager had a deeper need that had to be taken cared of.

Some weeks later, I saw him again.

"Guess what? You'll never believe it. My wife is sleeping perfectly now. She reads that New Testament you gave us, and falls right to sleep! See, I don't have eye bags anymore. And we don't fight as much, because now we're both getting the proper amount of sleep."

I celebrated with him. God showed His compassion on the post office manager's family.

WHEN YOU ARE ABOUT TO LOSE YOUR JOB...

The next day, I checked in at a different post office, one that was closer to our home. As I walked in the door, everyone stopped what they were doing.

"Ian, we saw you on the TV news! We didn't know you were a pastor. We just knew you as the nice Canadian guy."

They were so excited about the news program.

"Ian, I was so encouraged. I needed to know that there is hope for me. I needed to know that God has specific answers for me. And I came away from watching you on the news with the realization that there is help for me." said one.

One of the men asked me to pray for him, because he was about to lose his job. He did not have enough pension money to live on. He had a wife and children to feed at home.

Years later, I always see him at the post office every week. He never lost his job, and is doing a lot better financially these days!

I KNEW I HAD FOUND THE TRUTH

The headlines of several newspapers read, "Models are giving out New Testaments on the Streets of Turkey's Major Cities!"

All the girls on the team laughed when they saw those headlines.

One man wrote saying, "Today in Taksim, I saw the most beautiful girls in the whole world. They were giving out New Testaments. When she smiled at me, and handed me a New Testament, I couldn't help but want to become a Christian. This is the best missionary method ever."

One man wrote on a forum, "Today, I saw a model giving out New Testaments. As I stretched out my hand to receive the book, the model smiled at me. And that's the very moment that I knew I had found the truth."

You are created perfectly by God. And He likes how He created you. He is happy with all the gifts that He has given you. The talents you have are to glorify Him.

You look good. Your efforts are to be rewarded, thanked, and appreciated. He is proud of you. Keep doing what you're doing.

It is not small. It is significant. It is important. And it will bear results.

YOU ARE PROTECTED

When you work with the poor - be ready for anything.

It was a very dangerous part of town. Half a block away, two drug dealers sat in a black car. The youth would walk up to the car and the drug deals would take place. It's so dangerous that police are seldom seen in these areas.

We give out food packages to those who are sick and confined to their homes.

A young man jumped out from an alley, and grabbed my daughter Joy's arm.

My son Joshua is very keen. He spun around at that moment to face the guy who was holding Joy's arm.

Josh piercingly glared at the guy, and was about to push him. But before Josh could hit him, the guy fell back about one meter.

When he got up, he looked with a wide-eyed astonishment at Josh, and ran off.

From that day on, the entire community regarded Josh with a sense of awe. Nobody messed with us.

All that my son Josh did to the guy who was accosting his sister was turn around, and look at him! The guy fell over, and then ran off!

Josh is excellent at what he does. Joshua's keenness in security has saved us many times. And when you do what you're good at, God will do the rest.

Right now, you are being led to a higher level. You will be led into greener pastures. A good shepherd does his best for his sheep. His sheep are his livelihood. He wants them to be as well fed as possible. This ensures that he can have a greater return on his efforts.

There are times when you're the needy one. You might need a good break, or a download of mercy.

But when you are humble and ready to receive, you will go to the next level. What you sow, you also will reap.

Obedience will always keep you in the winner's circle. Because you have the potential to win, your courage, your strength, and your determination is to be celebrated. Your drive and passion for certain subjects and projects make you extraordinary.

People will want to help you. Mercy will come looking for you. I know favor will come your way. The very things that you need will jump out at you at any time, absolutely from anywhere. This is because you have been sowing seeds of goodness, and mercy, and kindness. These will grow to bring a harvest.

You've been created to be significant. You are a change maker. You will have the influence that you need. An average person you are not. You glorify God by going to the next level.

DR. IAN HERINGA

CHAPTER 16

THE GRASS IS GREENER ON YOUR SIDE

At one distribution event, a religious leader from a local mosque came and found us. He was wearing a long brown coat that flowed to his feet and trailed along behind him. His long beard and white skullcap set off the whole outfit. He cut quite a figure.

But there was anger in his eyes. Stalking each and every person that took their copy of the New Testament, he would pursue them. Walking alongside them down the street, he would scold them.

"What you are doing is wrong! It is against our rules to get that book! You will be eternally damned, and all the following curses will come upon you…"

He kept on rattling off a list of curses. Wow! This was a potential fire hazard!

We had been provided with a team of secret police by the Turkish government. They were assigned to protect us. They watched our every move.
As long as our long robed long bearded friend was on the street with us - there could be trouble. Never look for trouble!

SIT DOWN AND RELAX

We decided it was coffee break time. So we headed into Gloria Jean's coffee shop. Mmm..hmmm. That coffee was so good. It felt so good to just sit down and relax, while we waited for the religious leader to leave the area.

Our cell phone rang. It was the police who were our security. They were calling us. "Where did you guys disappear to? Come back outside. Are you guys afraid of the religious leader or what?"

"Thanks. But no thanks. We'll just finish our coffee and wait. There's no need to be out there right now. We're comfortable here in the coffee shop."

The police tried to convince us some more.

They dared us, "Oh! You cowards should really come out."

We replied that we don't need to be out there to create a scene. We didn't want a fight with the religious leader. We wanted to enjoy our coffee!

Eventually he left, and we went back to work.

ENJOY YOUR COFFEE

In the Bible, Jesus says, "Be slick as serpents, meek as doves."

Doves are all the time happy and can fly off anywhere, anytime. Doves are very hard to catch. They are always safe. Even if they land on the road, parking lot, or sidewalk – they never get stepped on or run over. Because when there is danger, doves simply fly away.

This is what it means to be meek as a dove. You don't have to fight every battle. Just turn the cheek, and fly off like a dove.

There are plenty of alternatives that are better and wiser for you. You need to understand what God is like. God wants you to live in peace. He will be the one to fight your battles. He doesn't lead you into trouble. He delivers you from trouble, into success and victory.

Recognize that you can be a peacemaker.

TROUBLE WILL AVOID YOU

The next day, we arrived back on the streets to give out God's message of love.

Three plainclothes police stepped out from a doorway. One was tall with a black leather jacket. He looked rather intimidating. The second police was short, overweight, and a baseball cap covered his balding head. The third police was rather sinister looking, pockmarks covered his face, and his teeth were yellowed from years of cigarette smoking.

The first policeman said, "Ian, today you are to set up your book table in a new area. Come with us."

I wondered what was happening. This would shut down the whole distribution. Nobody would be able to find us, if we weren't in the usual place that we were every year.

WHY FIGHT WHEN YOU CAN HAVE A FLIGHT

We followed the police, single file down the road, pulling our books with a trolley.

With every step, I became even more concerned. We always set up in the same spot each time.

"Oh well, we'll just make the best of the situation," I thought.

"Thank you guys," I said as the police left.

We went to work meeting people and giving out the new Testaments.

The minutes passed and I began to be suspicious about our new area.

Why had they removed us from our old area where we had been for years? I thought.

I looked around carefully. We came to realize that the alley around the corner was actually an inner entrance, a corridor entrance into the mosque!

And then it hit me! Today was Friday. It was a day when all good Muslims go to the mosque. People also lay their prayer carpets on the sidewalks, right on the street, all the way to the door of the mosque.

It was a set up for trouble! We were not sure why or who was behind this. But all I knew was that this was not a good idea.

The obvious plan that someone had cooked up was that we stay on the street on that Friday, and set up our stand (unknowingly on our part), right by the entrance of the mosque.

As Muslims gathered to do their prayers, they would see us.

Not a good scenario. We didn't want to offend anyone. We only wanted to give away the New Testaments to those who wanted them.

So we stopped. Our team did the dove routine (aka fly away). Why fight when you can have a flight?

JUST LET GO

Jesus did the same when they tried to throw him off a cliff. He slipped right through them, and went about his business.

You don't have to make things hard for yourself. Realize Psalm 23. He wants you to lie down in green pastures, beside still waters.

My friends and I went to bring a delivery of New Testaments to a bookstore.

Upon arrival, the storeowner was out. His assistant said he would be back in one hour.

We decided to wait for the storeowner to return.

As we walked across the square, a bearded, religious man with a skullcap appeared. He ran after me, and grabbed my bag of New Testaments.

He started pulling on the handle of the bag and shouting. He kept pulling and shouting. I kept a strong grip on the bag.

He would pull one direction, and I pulled back. I needed to hold onto my books! He kept pulling, trying to take the bag of New Testaments!

"I'm going to take you to the police!" He yelled.

We took turns, pulling back and forth. He was frantically pulling as hard as he could.

All of a sudden, I thought, "I'll just let go! This is getting tiresome. He can have them."

I let go, and turned to leave. He stared wide-eyed at me and a blank look came over his bearded face. He was so shocked! He didn't know what to do.

And then he ran after me, and gave me back my bag!

FLY UP HIGHER

God has multiple plans, multiple choices and opportunities waiting for you. He'll make sure that you fly up higher.

When you don't know what to do, God always has a plan. Even if your situation is difficult, painful, or dangerous, the pressure and turbulence will be used to push you higher. It will enable you to soar!

David was a shepherd boy. His job was to watch and care for his father's sheep. David was minding his own business, doing what he was good at.

Many days, the work was very slow. David would sit beside the stream and just stare at the clouds. Sometimes, he'd practice his slingshot.

One day, David's father called him. "David, I want you to bring these supplies to your brothers, who are fighting our enemies. Go to the battlefield, and bring them this food."

Often the battlefield looks so glorious to those who are watching the sheep. It looks so exciting and intriguing.

But David's time of looking after the sheep prepared him for what he was about to do.

When David arrived at the battlefield, what he saw made him angry. He saw the Philistine giant intimidating his own countrymen.

David began to plan in his head, and went to see King Saul. David saw himself as a warrior.

He had confidence from killing the bear and the lion. These predators had tried to kill his sheep – but David won!

Those previous battles made him confident and sharp.

ENJOY NATURE

As a Canadian, I grew up being outside in nature. I guess that is one thing that will never leave me. I love being outside.

Every week, different friends and I would wake up at 5:00 in the morning and head to the forest to pray. It was quiet and we'd all pick a favorite place to read our Bibles, and just reflect and pray.

There was no one to disturb us, no loud noises of traffic to distract us, and no computers dinging with new messages that need to be written and read.

That day, I had an especially good time in the quiet and solitude.

But my quiet reverie was broken, when out from the trees came soldiers. With guns slung over their shoulders, they shouted, "What are you men doing out here?"

"Good morning sirs. We are only out here praying," I answered.

"Yeah right. Like we are going to fall for that old trick. You are coming with us. You are under arrest," the soldiers said.

We were ordered to follow the old army truck to the command post.

As we sat in the office, I glanced at the report they were making out. It read, "We found these men praying in the forest to Jesus."

Yes, that is how I want to be described.

Oh and by the way, they eventually let us go. Their superiors found it funny that they had arrested us for praying. We left the command post having made new friends with the soldiers and their superiors.

THE PEACEFUL LIFE

Many times you find yourself waiting patiently by the stream like David with his sheep. You might feel insignificant, because the others are off, fighting the battle.

Not true! What you are doing is very important. And this is a special training time for you. Whenever David had free time, he did a lot of target practice, while relaxing and watching the sheep. He found that he had a talent for the slingshot.

He practiced and practiced and practiced. Many times, it seemed that he was only playing with his slingshot. However, it sure came in handy when it was time to fight off predators who came to attack his flock.

In times of peace, that is when we can excel and develop ourselves. Be grateful for the peace times.

PLAYING WITH YOUR SLINGSHOT

Wherever you are and whatever you are doing, you are important. As you watch your flocks and play with your slingshot, it is a very significant learning time.

David was to bring strength to the soldiers, who were intimidated by Goliath. He did not bring an academic degree, or a big financial plan to the battlefield. But what David brought was courage and faith.

God is developing you right now in what you're doing. Do not minimize the quiet and easy times. You are being equipped. You were not meant to be in battle the whole time.

Learn how to use that sling. Learn how to fight off the bear or the lion. And then you will be ready to take that giant down!

DR. IAN HERINGA

Part IV

Generous Goodness

DR. IAN HERINGA

CHAPTER 17

OVER AND ABOVE

One by one, the government was shutting down the four book companies that we helped set up. First Trent was deported out of Adiyaman. Then Kevin from Eastern Turkey had to leave the country because of lots of pressure.

The Ministry of Interior shut down my book company Meshur in Istanbul. Ben from Ankara was still open, but he had other troubles, like the molotov cocktail thrown in his office window. My friend Mario in Izmir was also having various reporters trying to give him trouble.

One day, I received a visit from the police. They handed me a notice that I was to report at the main police station. I was troubled.

What now? More problems? I thought.

That night, I didn't sleep. Pacing back and forth, back and forth, I prayed the whole night.

"God, help me. I don't know what is happening. I need to have news," I prayed.

While my wife and kids slept, I battled with the fear and dread that accompanies a summons to the police station. But as the sun came up, a new courage rose in my heart.

God is my present help in trouble. I repeated to myself as I walked up the marble steps, briefcase in hand. I made my way up to the correct office, paused on the steps to straighten my tie, and strode in.

"God, I have one request. I need to find out know what is happening with my file. Please give me favor," I pleaded silently.

YOU GOT THE INSIDE INFORMATION

"Good morning. I want to know what is the reason for my summons," I told the police man at the front desk. "I am a pastor of a church, and not a criminal."

They ushered me into another office. A young police appeared. He carried himself with a swagger that proved that he was a new recruit. "Ian, we have some questions to ask you," the young police said.

He slapped a folder on the desk and said, "This here is all the information we have on you. We know everything about you. We have been following you for a very long time. You are quite the man to keep an eye on," he said with a mean look.

The phone rang. "Yes, yes. Okay," the young police put down the phone and looked down his nose at me.

"You sir will wait right here. My superior is coming to interrogate you. And if I was you, I would pray hard, Ian," he laughed sarcastically.

He strode out of the room. I couldn't believe the opportunity that had just been presented. I grabbed the folder, walked fast down the hall and flew down two flights of stairs.

I ran to the photocopier. I handed it to the young boy who mans the photocopy machine. He slowly fed it into the machine.

"Oh God! Please don't let them come just yet. I can't get caught doing this!" I whispered.

I kept glancing at the door nervously.

Standing there at the photocopying machine, time stood still. At every footstep, I jumped and tried to hide the paper.

Finally, the photocopying was finished.

I ran back to the office, sat down, and placed the folder exactly on the desk. As soon as I had done that, in strode the superior officer.

My heart was pounding in my chest and I was still breathing heavily from having run down the hall and flights of steps.

The police looked at me suspiciously, and began asking me questions.

That night, Mary Jane and I gleefully went through the paperwork. That paperwork was extremely useful in the days that followed. We were able to use it as proof many times.

I asked God for information – He gave me the whole paperwork itself!

ASK FOR MORE

What would you ask God for?

When Peter went fishing, they couldn't catch any fish all night. (John 21)

Peter was so discouraged. But Jesus came along and told him to throw his net on the other side.

When the disciples threw their net on the other side of the boat, they caught an overwhelmingly large catch of fish. It was over and above all they had ever caught before.

When you ask God for something, be prepared to receive over and above what you had asked for. You need some overflow in your life.

This overflow is to help you get up again, and not let life beat you down.

Always be ready! You never know when you might get more than you asked for.

WANNA GO ON A TIGER SAFARI?

My beautiful wife Mary Jane is from the Philippines.

We had not been back to the Philippines, since our first year of marriage. That was over 20 years ago!

As a family, we made the trip to visit the multiple islands of the Philippines. Joy and Josh had never been to the country and original birthplace of their mom. It made for an incredible time!

One of the most memorable days was the tiger safari.

"Okay! Everybody climb inside the four-wheel-drive jeep," the guide called. We climbed in a strange looking vehicle. The four sides of the jeep were covered with an iron mesh. It was like being inside a cage on wheels. All 20 of us squished inside the jeep, and nervously huddled together. We had no clue of the horror and fright that we were about to experience.

Little did we know that we were about to be terrified.

The jeep driver brought a bucket of freshly cut chicken and put it next to him.

Slowly, the jeep made its way through the game park. We tried to see if there were any animals hiding in the tall grass, but none was to be seen. Our excursion brought us down a little pass, in between the trees, and out into the hot sunshine.

CAT FOOD

Soon, I saw what looked like a poster. It seemed to be a full-size poster of a large striped tiger staring at us.

It must be a poster. It has to be a poster. That tiger is standing too still to be real. I looked closer.

But it was real!

Snarl! It started to move towards us, creeping closer and closer to the vehicle. The driver threw a piece of chicken on a rope out of his window. As we waited, the tiger pounced on top of the jeep, growling as it showed its teeth. I thought could see its tonsils.

I stared in amazement. The rest of the group was screaming their heads off, staring, or kids just plain crying. The tiger opened up his large mouth. His teeth were just inches from my head, separated from my head by a metal mesh.

I could feel his breath. Ugh... He needed a breath mint or something.

Another tiger came leaping up at our jeep. Joy and Josh got tiger slobber all over their legs.

Then bang! A third tiger came along and jumped right on top of the jeep's roof. We could have touched the feet and claws of the tiger on top of the jeep. Not that anyone did. Or anyone wanted to.

"Aaahhhhh!!!!" Everyone screamed!

CROCODILE TEARS

We continued through the game park, tigers attacking our vehicle, eating the chicken that the driver would throw at them. These half-starved tigers were nothing like the lazy tigers I've seen at the zoo!

After we finished the ride through the big backyard of tigers, we jumped out of the jeep. Some of the little kids were still crying from fear.

We made sure everybody still had all their fingers and toes.

Our next stop was to visit the crocodiles. We walked over a long metal mesh bridge. Eight feet below the bridge were about 20 crocodiles.

The guide gave us each a long stick with a piece of fishing line attached. He helped us tie on chicken legs to the end of the fishing line. Our job was to feed it to the crocodiles.

Snap! The crocodiles would jump up, and snap their wide long jaws over the piece of chicken. And all we would be left with was the fishing rod and string, minus the chicken, and a shocked look on our faces.

Snap, snap, snap.

Feeding the crocodiles, seeing them jump and snap was quite the experience.

This was like no zoo I've ever seen! Most zoos say, "Don't feed the animals."

After feeding the crocodiles, we moved on to see some of the more tame animals of God's creation.

DR. IAN HERINGA

ENJOY THE EXOTIC

Live life big! Enjoy the exotic, take advantage of the new opportunities. Wherever you go and whatever you're doing, you will find something to add spice to your life.

God doesn't just want you to go to the zoo. He wants you to go on the tiger safari. Living life with God is always exciting.

When I first read about Turkey, I was intrigued by the culture, and by the strength of their people. Turkcy is my favorite place in the world, and Turkish people are my favorite people in the world.

Living in Turkey for so many years, I've had lots of adventures — above and beyond what I asked for. And to tell you the truth - it's been lots of fun!

YOUR HELP COMES IN ALL SHAPES AND SIZES

I needed to find a church. And it was turning out to be very difficult. Many landlords turned me down flat when they heard what I was going to use the place for.

"God, I need to find a church meeting place for us. I need a good neighborhood, one in which the neighbors will be comfortable with having a church in their area," I prayed as I drove through street after street, looking for "For Lease" signs.

Day after day, I'd drive through the streets of Istanbul.

When I got home, my wife would ask me how it went.

"Honey, it's going okay. But we have to pray. I don't know where we're going to find our church meeting place."

All night long, I'd pace the bedroom. This continued for weeks.

One day, I met one of the most curious characters I've ever met. His name was Cihan Bey. He owned a great place that would suit us perfectly.

Cihan Bey was always smiling. But it wasn't a happy smile, nor a sinister smile. It was something in between, like a tough grin. I just couldn't put my finger on it.

"Cihan Bey, I'm going to use this place for a church," I said.

I watched his face closely. Cihan Bey didn't even blink.

"Sure, sure. As long as you pay your rent on time," he wheezed.

That place turned out to be perfect. It was a great location, and easy for people to get to.

One day, Cihan Bey asked me to come to his office.

"Have you been having any trouble with anyone at all? Because if so, come to me. I'll take care of them. I rule this area with an iron fist." He pounded his fist on the table with such force, that I thought he might have cracked the table.

Cihan Bey looked up at me, smiled and said, "Want some more tea?"

THE IRON FIST

Then it all began to come to me. I began to understand the various people I'd meet in the elevator. Some were rich, some were so poor, and they would all come to visit Cihan Bey. It always puzzled me that even the police would come to pay their respects to Cihan Bey.

"Ha! I wonder if he is mafia! That's it." I said to myself.

After that, some of the team were rather scared of him. But he always treated us well.

It turned out to be the perfect location. Nobody gave us any trouble there. We were able to hold our meetings in peace. People were afraid to disturb us.

God gave us the perfect church, and the perfect landlord. Above and beyond what we asked for...

Even if he was mafia...

DOUBLE THIS, DOUBLE THAT

Job in the Bible went through many terrible trials. His children were killed, his flocks and herds were stolen. His thousands of oxen, donkeys, camels, and sheep were taken. He himself was covered with boils, a horrible skin disease.

But no! His situation was not permanent. Most Biblical scholars agree that this period in his life lasted for only a short time.

And at the end, Job got everything back – double!

He was vindicated with his friends and community. He ended up with double of everything. He got back double oxen, double camels, etc.

It was a total turnaround! I'm sure that it must have been quite a relief to Job. God gave Job more sons and daughters. His daughters were the most beautiful women in the country.

All his finances and investments in the form of flocks and herds were restored to him. He had double - twice as much as he had before!

THE BIG MISTAKE

It was the night before we were to leave for Canada. Actually, we had to be at the airport at 6:00 in the morning. It was already 11:00 at night. We were all packed, and ready to get some shut-eye for a couple hours, when suddenly Joshua exclaimed, "Dad! We don't have any chocolates to bring back to Turkey!"

"Oh no!" Everyone exclaimed.

We hopped in the car immediately. This was a crisis. For many years, our family would only come back to Canada every three years for 3 months. Chocolate was paramount on the list of supplies needed to survive.

Pulling in the parking lot of Walmart, I immediately decided that 24/7 Walmart stores were a blessing. Josh and I headed directly to the candy section.

It seemed we bought every candy we could ever want, or even wish for. The shopping cart had many bags of chocolates, and Josh made sure he got his sour gummy candies.

Feeling very pleased with ourselves, we pushed our cart to the checkout, and put everything in the car. I threw everything we had bought into a small suitcase in the back of the car.

Meanwhile, Mary Jane and Joy wandered around the store, picking up some last minute things. On their way out the door, they stopped by the candy section, and also bought chocolates!

When we got back to where we were staying, we all ran around making sure everything was packed. I took Mary Jane and Joy's stuff from Walmart, and threw it into another suitcase.

It was only when we got home to Turkey that we realized our mistake. Mary Jane and Joy had bought a whole small suitcase of candy, and Josh and I had bought another small suitcase of candy. We had doubled up!

Of course, Joy and Josh were very pleased with the big mistake. From then on, it seemed we were eating chocolate every day for a long time.

YOU NEED SOME MULTIPLICATION

Out in the middle of nowhere, Jesus and His disciples were healing the sick, and praying for people. After several days, the people became hungry and Jesus suggested that they be fed. But the only food to be found was a little boy's lunch.

This small lunch was prayed over. As it was given out to the people, it multiplied. Thousands of people were fed. Everyone had a good time together. They ate to the fill!

Get ready to be amazed at the multiplication of your provision. The little that seems to be there now is enough to be multiplied.

Generosity makes many friends.

What do you need multiplied?

DR. IAN HERINGA

CHAPTER 18

GOD IS PROUD OF YOU

Coming home to our apartment, I walked into the kitchen to make myself a cup of coffee. I turned on the tap, but no water came out! I came to find out that all our water, gas, and electricity had been completely shut off.

"Honey, what's up with the water? Since when has the water been off?" I shouted from the kitchen.

"Sweetheart, it's not just the water. It's the electricity and gas too," Mary Jane came into the kitchen.

"That means we don't have water, heat, or light in our apartment?"

I couldn't figure it out. Our utility bills are paid automatically from our bank savings account. After snooping around in the basement of the apartment, and asking our neighbors what had happened, I found out our landlord had manually shut off all the valves and switches in order to cut off our utilities.

I was shocked! The landlord had approached us two weeks ago, wanting us to lie to the tax authorities. The government was auditing him.

"Look, all you have to do is tell the authorities a different amount when they come and ask questions," he said.

I replied, "We can't do that. That would be wrong."

"Well, you'll just have to bear with the consequences of your decision then," he sneered.

PERISCOPE UP

I came home to find Mary Jane standing on the table by the window, with a periscope in her hand.

"Honey, what are you doing?" I asked.

"Shhhh… they're talking about us," Mary Jane whispered as she pointed to the garden.

We watched the landlord, and his cronies through the periscope, and listened to the conversation. They were plotting on how to evict us from the apartment, because we wouldn't lie for them!

This landlord made life difficult for us. He enlisted the help of our next-door neighbor, a lawyer. This lawyer began to try and intimidate us, day after day.

The lawyer would wait on his balcony for me to come home. Once in sight, the lawyer would threaten us. He would use all different types of tactics to get us to lie for the landlord.

"Look, I pay my rent every month. Why is he getting me involved in his personal tax problems? They are none of my business, and it would be wrong to lie," I said

We decided to move out. We quietly brought in a couple empty boxes everyday, and packed up the house. One evening after a late night at the office, I headed up the stairs to our apartment carrying a bunch of empty boxes.

I could hear the lawyer on the phone. He was shouting. I put one ear to his door, and listened. "You know that Canadian?" the lawyer was saying, "He is one smart cookie."

My heart jumped. I couldn't believe my ears at what I just heard.

LISTEN AND BE ENCOURAGED

Gideon was a young man who was afraid. But God had put a dream in Gideon's heart to deliver the Israelites from the Midianites. The Midianites were oppressing the Israelites every single day. But the Midianites were a massive army. But Gideon only had 300 men.

As battle day approached, Gideon was terrified. He knew there was no chance for his men to survive.

God said, "Gideon, go sneak down to the camp of the Midianites. I have something there that will encourage you. "

Gideon and his servant crawled on their stomach – all the way to the Midianite camp. The massive army was asleep. They came to the edge of the camp, and heard some men talking in a tent. Gideon crept up close.

"Last night, I had a dream. I had a dream that Gideon and his little band killed us all. I dreamt that they crushed us."

Gideon turned away with a smile on his face. And that was enough encouragement for Gideon to fight like crazy the next day. All the fear was gone. He developed a plan to use horns, the sound of breaking clay pots, and flashlights.

The Midianites thought that an army of thousands upon thousands of warriors had come upon them. The Midianites ran for their lives! Gideon and his small band of warriors won! They utterly crushed the Midianites – just like in the dream!

WINNING IS ENCOURAGING

The Lord knows that you need encouragement in order to win. His principle is not just a compromise. He wants you to conquer! God wants you to win, and win, and win, and win!

As you are encouraged, you will have creative ideas on how you can triumph. The Lord is fully aware of your needs. He is not hard and demanding. God does not expect you to run on without any help or hope.

Be assured that your victory is on its way.

Perhaps you need to remember the things that God has done for you in the past. Motivate yourself by remembering the times you won!

You see, success breeds confidence. The more confident you are, the more you can face your future head on. You'll be able to carry your family to see the victory that you have been aiming for. Whether you are rich or poor, successful or not, God is providing a way for you to see things in a different light.

So don't rehearse your failures. Don't let your shortcomings play over and over in your mind. Rehearse the good happenings and triumphs.

DON'T BE AFRAID

In the middle of the night, the police arrived at our house. Banging on the door and shouting, they woke us up. I came to the door in my pajamas.

"Yes? Good evening. Is there a problem, officer?" I asked.

The police just pushed past me, and began to search the house. They started walking around, looking into the rooms.

Joy woke up and started to cry. I held her in my arms throughout the whole ordeal. She was so afraid and hid her face in my shirt.

"Sirs, may I ask what you are looking for? What is happening? Why are we being searched?"

I received no answers from the police. Mary Jane and I stood back, as the police officers were looking through our house. I could see our neighbors peaking out of their doorways down the apartment building hall.

The police didn't find anything.

After what seemed like an eternity, the police finally left saying, "You are wanted for questioning at the police station tomorrow morning at 9 o'clock. Don't be late. We know where to find you."

The next morning when I awoke, I got up and looked in the mirror. Had it been a dream? No. I quietly gathered up my family and we all dressed in our Sunday best. We nervously headed for the police station.

The police station is huge. It is an imposing building, many floors high.

The police station is a place for criminals, lawbreakers, and swindlers - but not for families. Joy kept crying, so I carried her the whole time. We were so nervous and didn't know what to expect. Anyway, our hearts were peaceful.

Five police detectives began to question us. They asked me questions about God's book of love - the New Testament. Questions were asked about my past occupations, why I came to Turkey, and so on and so forth.

And when the turn came to question my wife, Mary Jane began to ask these men about the condition of their hearts. She talked about the importance of family. She explained the importance of being morally pure.

The policemen were stumped! They had never met a woman who had the courage to preach to them. These professional police detectives listened so carefully, and also hung their heads in shame as they were convicted about the kinds of lives that they were living.

And Mary Jane turned out to be the interviewer, the moral detective. The detectives were the ones who got interrogated.

It's a long story, but they eventually let us go again. We had to follow a whole legal process, which cleared our name, and was used as a precedent for other times that we were arrested.

YOUR ATTEMPTS ARE COMMENDABLE

You will fly above your past addictions, struggles, and fears. Remember, as you're hanging on to God - He is completely good. It is through God's goodness that you are being led and changed.

When you give of yourself, people get encouraged. When you make yourself available to serve, people get loved.

You've opened up your heart. You've sacrificed for your children. You've sacrificed to help your spouse in their career.

You've done whatever you had to do to make your family comfortable. You will be rewarded!

It's better to give than to receive. That's because you always get more in return. You are not forgotten. Your own dreams will get fulfilled.

The way you have been given of yourself to your job, your family, and to the causes that are important to you is very commendable. Just keep going!

Even if the dream seems impossible, that's okay. That means that it is a good dream. In this case, impossible is good.

God knows that you have it in your heart to help people. That's why He's opening up new doors for you. That's why He's letting you meet people who have also the same interests. That's why He'll make sure you meet the right connections in order to fulfill your dream.

He is proud of the way you work. The way you've been tackling new challenges makes Him smile with pride. Your persistence gets His attention.

God is proud of you – His child.

CHAPTER 19

EXCEPTIONAL HEALTH

Living and working in a foreign country with my family for 25 years now has posed many challenges, but also many encouragements.

Good health is a gift. Good health is a blessing.

And here is the punch line! In all our years of living in a foreign country, our family of four hardly got sick in Turkey, and didn't hardly have to see the doctors there.

And when my children did get sick, we would spend time praying and saw a lot of instant healings.

"God, I need to get to sleep. Please heal my babies," I'd pray.

One by one, we'd see the answers come. We have experienced

the gift of exceptional health!

In a small village in central Turkey, an elderly woman approached me. She wore the traditional baggy pants and headscarf, trimmed with crocheted flowers. A crowd of people trailed behind her, as she led the way towards our team.

"My son has arthritis in his leg. He's only 10 years old. It pains my heart to see him. He can barely walk."

The whole team gathered around the little boy. He was really a cute little guy. He shyly smiled at us, and then closed his eyes and opened his hands, as if to receive the prayer we were praying.

After we prayed, I said, "Hey little buddy, let's try walking again."

I grabbed his hand, and slowly walked him around the field. The little boy could walk perfectly!

He began laughing, "I can walk well again! It's not too painful anymore. I'll be able to play soccer again with the other boys."

The happy grandma looked at her grandson in shock! I smiled as I noticed the tears of happiness that were running down her wrinkled cheeks.

HORRIBLE GOITER, GO AWAY

"Please pray for my friend too," she said quietly. A man came out of the crowd, quickly opened his shirt to reveal a huge goiter on his neck. The mass was as big as a fist.

I thought, *Oh no! That goiter is horrible. What am I supposed to do with it?*

I reached out to touch it, and before I even got to it – the goiter disappeared! The crowd gasped! People looking from either side saw the goiter disappear.

The man touched his neck, touched it again. The goiter was completely gone!

The old grandma's family was being changed right there, right in front of her eyes. She began to sob. The whole clan gathered around and began to chant! A celebration broke out in the crowd. The grandmother led everyone as she raised her hands to heaven and began to chant, "Isa, Isa, Isa…" (which means Jesus in Turkish).

Our bodies can go through a lot. They are able to withstand a lot of stress. But yes, we all need some TLC – tender loving care.

That day in the village, we were reminded again to taste and see that God is good. He has solutions that are beyond your figuring out. He has answers beyond your calculations.

God sees your desperation and humility. That is what happened with this dear old grandmother. Because of her desperation, her grandson was healed of arthritis. And the young man's goiter shrank and disappeared! This is what you call the supernatural realm. This area is for God and God alone.

Wealthier people have more opportunities, and can pay for the best doctors and best hospitals. They might have many more solutions available to them. And of course God brings healing through doctors and medicine too. However, sometimes even all the money in the world cannot cure you.

Have you have run out of solutions? "No eye has seen, no ear has heard, no mind has conceived what God has prepared for those who love him." (1 Corinthians 2:9 NIV)

Sometimes people in the most difficult situations see the biggest miracles. That means you are eligible for miracles!

YOU ARE NOT A STATISTIC

A young lady saw our team walking down the street.
"Pastor! Pastor! Would you pray for my mother?"
The girl's voice trembled with emotion.
"She's blind."
We followed her down the street, and saw a big group of people having a picnic on the side of the road.
"Mama! Mama! The Pastor is here to pray for you."
We sat down on the ground, and a few family members gathered around.
"Ma'am, God loves you. It is not His best will for you to be blind. You are valuable to Him. You're not a statistic. He is deeply aware of your needs," I said.
"God, you know this woman needs to see," the team prayed.
And the woman saw! We did the whole "how many fingers" routine!

"I can see. I can see," she whispered over and over.

The old woman called her whole family to come. Over 50 people came, laughing, smiling – so happy!

At that point, everyone wanted prayer: for debts, for husbands who beat them, for their loved ones serving in the army.

They came to understand that God answers prayer; He is kind.

Accept God's kindness to you.

JUST LIKE PINOCCHIO'S NOSE

One of my legs was always shorter than the other. My right leg was about half an inch shorter than my left.

A friend of mine offered to pray for my leg.

"We need both Ian's legs to be the same length. That was your original plan for him. So God, we pray that Ian's right leg grows out to be the same length as his left," he prayed.

I stretched out my legs and before my eyes – I could see my right leg grow longer! Kind of like Pinocchio's nose.

I sucked in my breath. "Wow! Wow! Wow!" I exclaimed.

And now both my legs are of the same length. Perfectly.

COMPASSION IS GOD'S SPECIALTY

"He had compassion on them and healed the sick." (Matthew 14:14 NIV).

Compassion is God's specialty. God's bio of Himself is, "merciful and gracious, slow to anger, and abundant in lovingkindness and truth."

That is how God describes Himself throughout the Scriptures. Wipe clean any mental images of God that you have made previously. He is both strong and compassionate. Miracles happen because God feels for us.

DR. IAN HERINGA

Part V
Fulfilling Your Destiny

DR. IAN HERINGA

CHAPTER 20

ENRICHING LIVES

During one of our promotional events, the many requests for copies of the Turkish New Testament, God's message of love, began to overwhelm us!

The books were going out like hotcakes! It seemed like everyone and his brother wanted a copy of the New Testament. I noticed that we were getting low on books, so I grabbed one of the guys and went to go get more boxes.

We walked down the street to where the van was parked, just in time to see it being loaded up onto a tow truck.

"Hey! Hey! That's our van! Don't take it away!" I shouted at the top of my lungs. We started running in a panic down the street, as the tow truck started driving away with our van.

We frantically waved down the tow truck driver.

"Stop! Hey! Stop!" Without the van, there would be no more stock of New Testaments for the day.

One Turkish newspaper columnist wrote, "What would Christmas be in Turkey without the Christians giving out Turkish New Testaments."

Christmas would be ruined. Well, in our minds at least.

The tow truck driver obliged us by releasing the van. We still had to pay a parking ticket. One of my guys had parked our van in a no parking zone, of all places.

But yes, we had our van back. We had our books back. And Christmas wasn't ruined…!

LOVE IS THE WAY

You never know what things could happen to you, as you attempt to help people fulfill their dreams. As you touch the lives of other people, you yourself will be blessed extraordinarily.

Sometimes little problems happen. But they always remind us to be humble. Problems keep us from having the tendency to be proud and unfeeling.

No matter what happens to you, know that God is for you. Keep your shoulders back, hold your head up high, and expect everything to work out for good.

When the unexpected problem comes your way, this may be the time to refocus. You may need a slight adjustment in your agenda or schedule, which will make all the difference.

Welcome the trials and difficulties. If you are humble, God will speak to you through those very trials. You'll get extra understanding, extra motivation, and more than you could ask or even think.

Having been arrested over 50 times, I sometimes could feel bad for myself. But even now, I am seeing how God uses each and every time to help me.

I'm challenged to give more, show more mercy, be kinder and be more loving!

HERE'S LISTENING TO YOU

Every Sunday, just before church is about to start, Cemal shows up. A tall older guy with a military bearing, we always greet him politely when he comes. I greeted him, gave him a hug – and that's when I felt a gun hidden at his waist.

Cemal is a curious character. He's always polite. He's always punctual. But he never prays or participates. He just sits there on a chair, always watching.

Oh yes, back to the story. Cemal is a nice fellow. We try to forget the two items that he always brings along with his Bible: his gun, and a listening/recording device. Cemal is a spy, a government informant sent to monitor all our activities.

DON'T SAY, "OH NO"

We could get all stressed out about Cemal's coming. It is rather nerve-wracking. Or we could start complaining, and become fearful about his presence in the church service.

But the best thing to do is to let it drive us higher. You'll become more discerning, more careful in what you say and what you do. You'll learn to be kinder, to understand people better. It also helps as a motivation to give more of yourself.

I never knew if Cemal was recording or not. But when he goes back to his superiors, I knew that they would be hanging on my every word and preaching. Or to put it the other way, I might be hanging from my every word.

Every Sunday, it seemed that we have a practical course on how to love your enemies.

I had to act it out. I had to be loving and kind every single week. My life depended on it.

Cemal was a nice guy on the outside for sure. But I sure didn't trust that gun of his. Sometimes he'd bring a friend. That was even worse.

Your destiny is great. The difficulties are here to help get you to the top of your game.

It was also an exercise to keep the staff in the church peaceful and happy - in spite of the gunslingers present in our services.

The way you walk with courage, and boldness, and with joy in your step will affect how your family or team follows you. It will affect everyone around you.

WINNING

In the Bible, Nehemiah had similar problems. He had three guys who were constantly criticizing him and his project.

Nehemiah had a dream to build a wall around the city of Jerusalem.

It seems that Nehemiah's three enemies got a bit discouraged after a while.

So they hired another fellow to help try and defeat Nehemiah. The new guy's job was to spy and question everything that Nehemiah did. I guess Nehemiah's enemies felt that they were short staffed.

This is so true! No matter how many people you have against you – they are all the time short-staffed.

You are the majority. No one can stand against you all the days of your life.

That means Monday, Tuesday, Wednesday, and the rest of the week. It even means for the rest of the month... and so on, and so forth.

Enemies can try to stop your endeavors, but ultimately enemies will only boost you to a new level of increase. In the Bible, Paul told Timothy to "fight the good fight". You see the fight you are in is actually a good one.

You might not find any good fights on TV, or in the newspaper. The only good fight you will find is the one that you are in! As you do what you know best to do – you will win.

You might say, "Well, I have a lot of people against me…." Congratulations! That means your next promotion should be even bigger.

Just keep hanging in there, and remember that yours is a good fight.

WORKING THROUGH THE NIGHT FOR YOU

I remember the time my team was arrested. Wow! That was a challenge getting them all out of jail. This is how the story went...

Mert, Mucahit, Muammer, and Hande went to a park to do surveys. We needed some specific market research regarding people's reading interests. And if you completed the survey, you were given a chance to enter for a Turkish New Testament. In this way, we ended up distributing thousands of Turkish New Testaments as well. Two birds with one stone!

While doing the surveys in the park, a police patrol stopped them. Mert, Mucahit, Muammer, and Hande were shoved into a police car. The three Turkish guys, and one girl were sent on their way to a Turkish police station.

At the police station, they called me. "Ian, we got arrested. Please help us! Please get us out of here."

Oh no... the team is in jail. I thought.

I went home first, grabbed my best suit (the suit that I had been married in), and wore my best tie. Combing my hair, I tried to look as prepared as possible in the mirror.

KEEP GOING

Arriving at the police station, I announced, "I am Pastor Ian. You have my employees here. I demand their immediate release, or I will call the embassies."

The police clerk stood up from his desk, and said, "I'm sorry, sir. Your employees have already been transferred to the main police station."

Heading downtown, I quickly found a parking space and headed for the front door of the police station. I threw my shoulders back, straightened my tie, and ran in.

But as soon as I walked in the door, a policeman got on his radio and said, "Come quick! These Christians are multiplying!"

After some cajoling, I was given permission to speak with Mert, Mucahit, and Muammer. Hande had been sent to the women's jail.

"What happened guys?" I asked

"Well, we were just standing there in the park, trying to decide where to go next, when the police began shouting at us. They told us to come with them, and they put all of us in the police car. It was so stressful, Ian. We prayed under our breath, just like you do when you are in trouble. But anyways… do you think you can get us out soon?" The guys were clearly not happy with their new living arrangements.

Muammer had been slapped on the face several times. Mert had been beaten and kicked.

I right away got on the phone to Mary Jane who immediately called the embassies.

I headed home, picked up my wife, and we prepared to stage a sit-in protest (well, not quite) at the police station.

But when we arrived there, the police had moved Mert to another holding cell in a different area of town.

THE SEARCH IS ON FOR YOU

The whole night long, we went from one police station to the next, looking for Mert.

"Is Mert being held here?" We'd ask.

"No, he's not here." We checked police station after police station. It was one long night.

Mary Jane kept calling the embassies.

When things don't work out sometimes, you just need to keep on keeping on. Many times the people who get to the top get there, because they are the ones who didn't quit. You have what it takes to keep on.

You might feel like you're the last one still singing your song. Just keep on singing.

There's a reward waiting for you.

We finally found Mert. As for Hande, she was taken to a different jail as well.

In her jail cell was a hooker. Hande was able to love the girl, and be a listening ear. They talked about the different difficulties the young hooker was going through. Hande was able to help her have a new outlook on life.

The hooker began to pray to Jesus for a new life. This was wonderful!

Later, Hande said it was worth spending the night in a cold prison cell for the sake of her new friend.

Finally in desperation, I made a midnight call to a friend who worked at the American embassy. He made a couple calls, and got his people to call the Turkish police.

By about noon the next day, everybody was released.

THE LOVE LAW

Maybe you are finding yourself face-to-face, and in close contact with someone with whom you don't agree. You might not see eye to eye with them. However, you have many good things to offer. You will be a change agent in the lives of these other people.

Don't focus on the differences. They probably just have a different lifestyle than you do. Focus on who you are and what you have to give. You are an incredible person who can extremely bless everyone around them.

There are times when you have to fight for others at your own expense. This type of fighting is different than fighting your own good fight. This type of fighting means you lay down your life. Sometimes sacrifice is the acid that will dissolve the chains for someone else.

That someone else is always worth it. God is no respecter of persons. He regards every person with extreme value. When you put up with, and build up someone else - you are acting on a deeper law of life than many people understand. It's the law of love.

BUILDING A BETTER COMPANY

As the demand for God's book of love increased, so did our demand for more staff. We first opened up the Meshur Distribution Company.

Meshur provided a legal framework through which staff could be trained and motivated. The distribution company gave us many more platforms through which to encourage, and build up others.

By this time, God's book of love was going out by the thousands - to prisons, libraries, schools, and stores...

HELP OTHERS TO SUCCEED

Together, my wife Mary Jane and I knew we must give of ourselves to help others to be successful. Many more people needed to get God's book of love.

Next we opened up another distribution company in the city of Ankara together with Ben. Ben is a close friend of mine from Asia, and is an unstoppable go-getter. We loved his passion and energy.

One morning, Ben headed to the office. As he opened the door, he was welcomed to his office by a molotov cocktail! The damage to the office was severe.

Kevin, another good friend, had been working with me in Ankara, and wanted to give out God's book of love in the city of Mersin.

We started another distribution company in Mersin with Kevin. For a long time, we funded different promotional events in Mersin, Ankara, and Izmir.

Then we helped Trent. Trent and I started a distribution company in Adiyaman.

Mario did excellently in Izmir and we were faithful friends as well. He is a bold, charismatic person!

It was very busy for all of us. Everyone was very motivated to work in each different area of Turkey.

When you hold things loosely, they can multiply faster. As we help each other, it is very rewarding. The dream will grow.

Each person is gifted differently. Each person will operate the company better, if it's done according to their gifting. The result will be a better company.

Together with various other means and strategies, we saw over half a million New Testaments distributed in every single province, and major city in Turkey.

PTL!

TRULY LOVED

Soon Kevin, in his pioneering spirit wanted to move to the city of Malatya. In this new city, he needed more copies of God's book of love, the New Testament.

We packed up 1000 books and shipped them right to him. The shipping company called the media, and created a whole scandal about the minister who had just moved to Malatya with his family. After a year or two and many different troubles, Kevin was forced to leave Turkey with his family.

Six months later, we were watching the evening news. The banner at the bottom read, "BREAKING NEWS: Three Christians have been martyred in the city of Malatya".

We were horrified as these words scrolled across the screen.

These three precious believers were horribly murdered in the old office. The sacrificial and exemplary lives of these 3 men shook the whole country.

Everyone was in dismay. The newspapers wrote that the real target had actually been Kevin. We grieved for many months for our brothers in Malatya.

The only way that these three brave Christian men in Malatya could lay down their lives was because they knew the true love of God.

They truly loved others.

YOU ARE A BRAVE SOUL

I received a call from Nuri. He lives in Van city, in Eastern Turkey. It is close to the Iranian border.

Nuri ordered many copies of God's book of love. He wanted to know about love.

Nuri was of was Kurdish descent. He told me how he struggles with many feelings of rejection, insignificance, and low self-esteem.

"No one is helping my people. We are forgotten."

I assured him that, "No, Nuri. You are not forgotten. In fact, you are a champion. You are a leader among your own people. And I want you to know that you are a brave leader. No one can take that away from you. You are a person that is not forgotten."

NOT FORGOTTEN

Tens of thousands of Kurdish people had fled from the regime of Saddam Hussein. They were all living in tents on the Turkish Iraqi border. With no food or water, the situation was dire.

A church in England collected clothes, blankets, and supplies to give to the Kurds. I drove with them together to the city of Van. And from there, we were to go to south to the Iraqi border.

We pulled up with 5 vehicles in front of the hotel. The hotel was bustling with activity. Aid workers with clipboards ran here and there. The humanitarian crisis had drawn NGO's from all over the world.

I was about to head into the hotel, and try to make some contacts and see if we could stay there.

I got the shock of my life, when Nuri stepped out of the doorway.

"Ian! How are you? Do you remember me? I met you a long time ago."

"Of course I remember you. That was three years ago," I replied as I gave him a hug.

"Ian, I never forgot those words that you told me."

"Well Nuri, I have something to show you. Come with me."

So I showed him the trucks that were full of supplies.

I said, "Look Nuri. We have come to help your people."

HELPING THE UNDERDOG

This is your chance. You've been prepared for this time. Being an underdog yourself, you have been given a chance to recover.

And now, please believe what I have just said. Take time to look in the mirror and rehearse your history. Remind yourself of who you are, and where you have come from.

You will find no greater joy and fulfillment, as you give of yourself to develop others. As you build successes into the lives of others, all your own dreams will come true.

When you give of your life to others, this is a very precious thing, Keep doing it!

Live deeply, live to multiply, give sacrificially.

HITTING THE BULLSEYE

One thing about the poor is that they are very humble. They know they need help.

The poor are people in desperation. That means you and I can fit into that category.

One dear lady in the slums said, "No one comes to help us but you Christians," weeping softly, she was expressing her gratefulness.

Every week, we would bring chicken and bread. Having meat to eat was a treat for the poor families! Feeding the poor is difficult because they have nothing. They do not have jobs. They do not have healthcare, or the proper places to live. Their homes are made out of cardboard and plastic. Their clothes are ragged, the children don't go to school, and the parents go through the garbage to make a living.

When you take time to help the down and out, the single mom, the rebellious student, or the skid row veteran, you are not expecting to be paid back by them.

Remember to fight for others! You are on the right track when you're doing these things.

You've hit the bull's eye.

You have hit the home run.

You've received your degree in life. Congratulations.

PEOPLE NEED PEOPLE

There will be times when your boss asks you to work overtime. When you've been divorced, you might have to work harder to see and be with your children.

Listen to a friend who is hurting. And standing up for a person.

who is being oppressed will truly be worth it. Helping a single parent, helping the elderly, this is what life is about.

People like to be independent. But at some time or the other, we all need help. There are no exceptions to this rule. Everyone will have a time when they cannot help themselves. And that is when true friends step in.

You cannot insulate yourself from the human race. If you live on an island, you still need someone to bring you food. If you live in the North Pole, you still need someone to remind you to turn out the lights. No matter where you live or what you do, people need people.

Don't miss your opportunity to give; it could make history!

CHAPTER 21

YOU'RE ALMOST THERE

We were stuck! Wheels spinning in the mud, I tried to maneuver our vehicle out of the slime. With the back of the car filled with New Testaments, we were in a precarious situation.

In the middle of the night, and out in the middle of nowhere, the military ruled this area with an iron fist. No telling what they would say, if they saw the boxes of New Testaments in the trunk. Although the New Testament is legal in Turkey, it was always a toss up on whether we would get arrested or not.

On our way to a city in the East to deliver New Testaments, we drove onto the side of the road to change drivers. When we got back in the car, it wouldn't budge.

Everyone got out. I tried to maneuver the car out of the mud. But the mud just pulled our car in deeper. And then the engine totally died. We almost gave up too.

"Guys, this is a serious problem…" I said.

As we sat down on the side of the road, a big dump truck drove up.

A man jumped out of the cab on crutches and said, "Boys, what's with the downcast faces? You stuck?" He asked inquisitively.

We just pointed to the car in the mud.

"Well boys, I can fix that," the dump truck driver said with a grin. "We'll drive your car right into my dump truck and get it out."

The dump truck driver's name was Ercument. He drove with a stub foot. He had escaped from a horrific accident, which had severed his foot.

"Driving is the only occupation I can do," he explained. "But tonight, I am your miracle! You won't have to stay the night in the cold and get eaten by the Turkish wild dogs," he chuckled.

I got in the driver's seat of the car, and the others pushed the car into the back of the dump truck.

But then the truck's back tires began to spin in the muck. So we had a broken down car, sitting on a dump truck that was stuck in the mud!

A military jeep drove up and saw that we were in trouble. The soldiers blocked off the highway, stopping traffic on both sides. The jeep pulled the truck out of the mud safely onto the highway.

In all the excitement, I realized I couldn't open the car doors to get out of the car. The car and I were tightly wedged in the dump truck. So I stayed in the car, while the truck drove all of us to a mechanic's garage in a city two hours away. I couldn't see anything. But I knew we were moving because of the bumps in the road!

YOU WILL BE RESCUED

The path to your destiny might look like you are stuck, spinning your wheels in the mud. Or it may even seem that you are stuck in the truck that is stuck in the muck.

Please don't stop trying. Right now, God is sending people your way to pull you out. His heart is completely for you. Don't believe all the lies of addiction, all the lies of debt, all the accusing voices that are telling you that you're not good enough. Your help is on the way!

Even if you can't see where you are going, you are being carried to your next level. When you feel that you're at a job going nowhere, or can't even find a job – don't feel worthless. When you feel like your marriage is disintegrating – you are still very precious in God's eyes.

Your passion to do more, to have a better position at work, to earn more money for your family, to improve your relationships is to be applauded. Your desire and determination is so valuable.

You are a person of quality - that won't stop. There is something in you that is burning for more. This is what makes you different. Don't condemn yourself by saying, "I'm not where I should be."

The fact that you haven't quit is undeniable. Your fire is still burning. You have an unmistakable quality that has been refined in the fire of daily monotony.

You are ready for more. You are the stuff that success is made of. Just hang tight. Keep believing and expecting. You are soon to arrive!

Your expectation is about to turn into reality. Your reward is on its way. God is about to step in and turn your faithfulness into your dream. He's going to open up the back of the dump truck, and you will find yourself suddenly at your destination.

HAPPY IN YOUR COMING AND GOING

I remember when my application for a long-term visa was revoked, time and time again. We ended up leaving the country of Turkey when my visa would run out, and then entering again – every three months. It was a grueling trip, but one that had to be made.

This time, we were headed to the Bulgarian border. After hours of waiting in the line up at the border, it was finally our turn. The border guards checked our documents, and we found ourselves leaving Turkey, and entering Bulgaria.

After spending some time sightseeing, we returned to the border in order to reenter Turkey.

Again, there was a long line up of trucks and cars. We sat there and waited.

We ended up waiting a long time in our car. The night was cold and we ran the car engine every so often, just so we could feel our fingers and toes again.

We finally arrived at the border guard's booth to buy our Turkish visas. The border guard looked at my passport, looked at me, then back at my passport. He clicked around on his computer for a while, with a puzzled look on his face.

The border guard radioed his superior. They both looked at my passport, then at my face, then back to the passport.

There was some commotion inside the booth of the border police. I strained my ears to hear what they were saying. But I couldn't quite make it out.

The border police knocked on our window. He had a very stern look on his face, as he ushered us into the main building there at the border crossing.

"What is happening? Why is there such a delay? Is something wrong?" I asked him quietly.

His answer shocked me.

"We are under orders to arrest you and bring you to the nearest police station."

I was floored.

"Why? I am a Canadian citizen and I have been living in Turkey for over 20 years now." I said.

"I cannot tell you why we are arresting you. Those details are not accessible to you. We have to follow our orders," the stern police said.

IN BETWEEN COUNTRIES

We were scared. It was the middle of the night, and these border guards were none too friendly. The others had been cleared to reenter Turkey. But I was the one who had a big problem. They wouldn't let me back in, and on top of that, I was to be arrested and brought to the nearest city's police station.

As we waited again, an old woman and a young man made there way towards us.

"Do you need help? We can help you [wink, wink]. For the right price, we can smuggle [wink, wink] you into Turkey."

My only thought was, *I wonder if they take Visa or MasterCard.*

All of us were praying fervently. By this time, it was already getting to be early morning. Everyone was tired.

I prayed for a miracle.

In fact, it was only a miracle that would get me out of this situation. I had already tried every other way I could think of to talk my way out of this situation with the police.

Just then a phone call came through. The policeman looked at me, talked some more, and then looked at me again. He hung up the phone, wrote something on the computer, and stood up from his desk.

"You are free to go," he said.

"I'm free to go?" I replied. I didn't stay long enough to ask what had just happened. I ran out of the office, jumped in the car, and we went roaring off to Istanbul.

We had once again reentered the land that we love so much. I wondered what that phone call was about. And as everyone fell asleep, and I drove through the night, I realized how thankful I was to be free.

DESPAIR IS NOT YOUR FRIEND

When you think things are not going as smoothly as you had hoped, don't feel bad about yourself. Don't lose hope. Don't stray from your original vision.

You've already come this far! There is more to come for you. Right now, there can be things grabbing at you, trying to take your time, your money. There could be things trying to steal your reputation, or your peace.

Don't despair.

You are being prepared for a greater level in your business.

You are being trained to be an encouragement to a lot more people.

The Apostle Paul wrote many of his letters from a jail cell. These letters make up a large part of the New Testament. Difficult situations can be turned to good use.

NO CLOSED DOORS FOR YOU

Small dreams grow into big dreams. Big dreams might seem impossible. But big dreams become possible through many little steps. When you feel that the door is closed, and the room is closing in on you, it is not that way at all.

You see, the little door that you see may be closing in on you. But will you believe in your dream enough, to see the big door opening up for you?

You may need some time to plan again, and get a fresh take on things. You might need to find some more like-minded people to help you. But you are unstoppable. No one can take you out of the race.

Know your part. Carry your dream. Keep the dream alive. And by doing that, your dream will multiply all by itself.

Don't measure your achievements with anyone else. Yours is a different dream. Don't try and measure water with a measuring tape. It won't work. Don't measure the amount of gas you have in your tank, by trying to look inside the filler tank. Look at the gas gauge. The Lord will give you encouraging signs. Stay in faith!

The point is that there are no closed doors for you. Everything may not happen the way you want it to, but that's okay. There are other ways.

HOW TO SELL A CAR IN AN IMPOSSIBLE MARKET

We had to sell our car. And yes, we had a Turkish man who wanted to buy it. We didn't know it at that time, but Turkish government had a ban on all foreign car sales until further notice. We went from one registry to another. Some clerks said they could do it, but then sent us to a different registry. And that registry would say the exact same thing, and on it went.

The man who was going to buy the car became angry. As we drove down the road to the next registry, he began to shout at me.

"You foreigner! You are wasting my time. I'll buy your car, but only for half of what we previously agreed on."

He continued to rant and rail. I tried to placate him, but he was too angry.

He finally shouted, "If you don't sell your car to me for half price – you better watch your back. Now let me out of the car, let me out of the car, or I'll kill you!"

Whoa! What a temper that man had. I was pretty glad we didn't have to deal with him anymore.

I didn't know what to do. We had just lost our one and only buyer.

But in faith, I traveled to the other side of Istanbul, to the main traffic building to inquire how I might sell that car.

KEEP DOING THE BEST YOU KNOW HOW

No matter how many mistakes you make, today might be full of temptations, but you are still doing your best. Others may be jealous and make life hard for you, your life may be falling apart, but you are still doing your best.

You might not have all your i's dotted, and your t's crossed exactly the way other people want it done, but just keep doing the best you know how.

Keep moving ahead. Don't look to the left or to the right. Keep going. Because your best is about to become better.

Did anyone ever tell you that you are improving at an incredible rate? It's true. You might not believe it, but that's only because you can't really see yourself.

Look back on your life. You are improving. You are doing better than you were 5 years ago, or even six months ago. Some things might not be so great right now, but at least you are wiser.

It's okay if other people are ahead of you. There are other people running behind you.

Don't look to the right, or to the left. But just don't let anyone be whispering in your ear, while you're running. The very fact that you're running will demonstrate results.

Even if all you get is a T-shirt at the end, that says you were in the race, you are still a marathon runner.

You know that you are a runner. And that is good enough.

THERE IS ALWAYS A WAY

Istanbul is a city of 10 million people. You cannot imagine the traffic. Sometimes on the highway, all you can see for miles ahead is cars, more cars inching their way forward in traffic. My friend and I made our way to the main traffic building, and found our way to the office of those who are in charge of car sales.

"Sir, we have to sell our car. How do we do that? Some registries are telling us that they can do it, but when they try – the registry system won't let them."

"Look, all you can do is wait. The government has put a hold on all foreigner car sales. All you can do is wait," they repeated.

My friend and I found a five-star hotel, situated ourselves in the lobby, and started to call each and every used car salesman we could find in the yellow pages.

We must have called at least 30 dealers. A few of the stores said they would buy the car for a ridiculously low price. Most gave us a flat out no, when they heard we were foreigners.

But then, we found one that said yes! And on top of that, they would buy our car for the amount we wanted.

We headed back to the other side of Istanbul again. But when we arrived at the store, the owner said, "Look, I'm sorry. But I can't buy your car. I'll buy it for 40% less, though."

I was so disappointed. We visited a couple more car dealerships. Everyone said no. Many told us it would be impossible for us to sell our car. No one would buy a foreigner's car, while this government ban on foreign car sales was in effect.

But when we had lost all hope, we met a friendly car salesman and his sons. They agreed to buy our car – for a right price too! We literally danced out of their store.

When you have tried as many open doors as possible, and have found no results - what do you do? You can try again.

Just remember to never give up. The very time you are about to quit could be the time that you will succeed.

Don't forget that all your efforts are admirable efforts. You have been doing your best, and you have been eagerly waiting to see the results. The results will come. You have been standing in faith and dealing with integrity. And most of all, you have been trusting God.

Now don't be amazed at the incredible opportunities that will present themselves to you. If you quit now, you will never know the results that were about to be put on your plate.

Your efforts will soon become fruitful. Every step that you take up a mountain means one step higher, and one step less to go. You are one step closer to your victory.

PERSEVERANCE IN YOUR DNA

Where there's a will, there's a way. God guides the steps of the righteous. You are a survivor, and an overcomer. You have perseverance in your DNA.

There is no going back - that is not who you are.

"You are awesome in the eyes of your enemies," is what God says about you. During difficult times, your creativity comes to the surface, and the new thing is born.

RUN YOUR RACE

Finally, the car was sold! This was already close to the end of the day.

We jumped in a taxi and got to the bank, just as the guard was locking the bank. We knocked on the window, and the guard let us in. I burst through the doors of the bank, and we deposited the money. Hooray!

I knew that God was with me. I felt the fresh breeze of success in my sails.

In the Bible, Paul tells us that we are to run the race in such a way as to get first prize.

That means God wants a whole crowd of winners. He sees each one running his own race, and winning. Each one of us is to be congratulated for our efforts, for our stamina, and giving God the glory for the success.

The first prize is not as elusive as it looks. Gaining that place in the winner's circle is what has been put in your heart. You actually like winning.

You might not have all the experience, and the education, and the finances. It's okay that there have been roadblocks. You have not been disqualified. You are not late. Your faithfulness is something that is actually quite rare. The Bible says a faithful man is hard to find.

There is a way through for you!

DR. IAN HERINGA

IT'S A HAPPY LIFE

CHAPTER 22

YOU ARE WELL ABLE

The President of Turkey was coming! The security was extremely tight. Police set up barricades all over the place in preparation for the President's arrival and speech. Excitement ran high as everyone gathered to line the streets, hoping to catch a glimpse of the President.

On our team, we had a guy named Yildirim. He came from a poor family, and Yildirim himself was always in debt. But one day, Yildirim realized that God is his provider as well as his Savior.

With that realization, slowly but surely – Yildirim began to be able to pay off his debts. His finances stabilized, and he felt so free!

Because his own life had been so transformed, he had such a

passion to tell people about it. He would tell everyone how they could have the strength to get out of debt and be happier. He had a passion for his country and wanted to see poverty eliminated. Yildirim also had the desire to one day be able to give a New Testament to the Turkish President.

That day, as the town prepared for the President's visit, Yildirim was in the right place at the right time. He slipped through the crowd, right up to the front. It was just a flash moment. And Yildirim somehow found himself face to face with Turkey's President.

"Mr. President, this... this is for you," Yildirim stammered.

He handed the President a red Turkish New Testament.

Giddy with happiness, Yildirim sat down in the stands.

"I can't believe it! I did it! I did it! I really gave the President the Book." Yildirim exclaimed.

He waited for the President's speech to begin. Scanning the dignitaries, he quickly picked out the President. And look! The President was reading the New Testament in the Presidential Box.

GOD SEES YOU THROUGH

What is your story? What is your dream? And who needs to hear it?

Joseph was hated by his brothers, and sold as a slave, yet he was destined to become prime minister of Egypt.

Esther was a young Hebrew girl who became Queen, and saved the Jews, her people, from genocide.

Peter was a simple fisherman, who later became one of the main leaders of the church.

You are who you are for a purpose. Your dreams, and your passion will carry you through every storm, and every desert. You have the necessary gifting. Opportunities will come looking for you. You will be amazed!

Why did God take Yildirim from living in a shack, and place him right in front of the President of Turkey with a message? The answer is because God wanted to target two birds with one stone.

God wanted to encourage Yildirim. He wanted to let him know

that he can be fearless, and become a mighty man of God. And God wanted to also encourage the Turkish President. The President needed to read God's message of love.

God is great. God is awesome. So if you are connected and submitted to Him - why shouldn't your life be spotted with awesome and sprinkled with great?

Today is the day that God has made! You can be full of expectancy today.

Worrying about tomorrow will wear you out. Just live your life moment by moment – being that exceptional person that you are. God did not create some people to be normal, and some people to be exceptional.

No! Your life started with a dream – a big dream that needs to be fulfilled.

No one can hold you back. I am excited for you. We will be able to look back together, and stand in amazement at the wins you have scored. And you will receive the courage to face your future.

We only have so much time on earth. Use your days with great purpose and passion. Don't use your days to feel bad about yourself, and live in a perpetual pity party.

Who knows? You may be the only one with the key to help others with a specific problem they are facing.

.

YOU HAVE HEART

You might be saying, "How can you say that to me? I'm not like that."

No. It is not just me talking to you like that. It is God talking to you like that. He has put such powerful vision, and potential in you. On top of that, you have heart.

And heart makes all the difference.

You are unstoppable, and that is what's unique about you. That is why we are told to run the race, with such passion and purpose. You can get the first prize!

That is Bible truth, my friend. Whoever you are, that first prize is waiting for you, and you alone. If you seek God, you will find Him.

The flip side of it means that God is the one who does the

finding. He'll still find you even if you aren't being that diligent in your seeking. The Finder is greater than the seeker.

Trust in God, and as you trust, you will be amazed. Trust, and you will never be let down. Trust, and you will be renewed, refurbished, and encouraged!

WHATEVER HAPPENS, YOU MEET THE QUALIFICATIONS

After finishing Bible School at Prairie, I felt it was time for me to pack up my family, and live in Turkey. I began my application process.

First, I met with the church missions board. At that time in my life, I was very shy and quiet. I nervously told the committee of my desire to live in Turkey and help people there.

After I set forth my proposal, I had to wait while they discussed it. After a while, they called me back in. Apprehensively, I walked into the room.

"Ian, at this time we do not feel you are ready for such a task. There are certain things in your life that you need to develop, before you take your family, and work in Turkey. Frankly, you do not entirely meet our qualifications."

I was crushed.

That was that.

And you know what? It was true too.

I knew it in my heart.

I was quite shaken. *What is wrong with me? What should I do? How should I change?* I had to respect the comments of the committee and knew that they were right in a sense.

I didn't have what it takes. I came to realize that.

I didn't fill the prerequisites. I couldn't be labeled as a "missionary extraordinaire."

I struggled through a lot of things.

But after more than 20 years of trying, now the Religious Affairs Department of the Government lists my ministry on their website as a main Christian work and strategy in Turkey.

YOU ARE BELIEVED IN

When your Heavenly Employer looks at you, He sees the finished product. He knows that you can do it. He doesn't worry about you not matching up with the finished product. You are in process. You already have it in you.

He will hire you, because of His immense love for you, which equals his immense belief in you. He will move people around, so that Yildirim from a shack can be encouraged when he meets the President, and presents a New Testament to him.

God knows you have what it takes. He will move people around for you. He'll make sure that you are encouraged to have a greater faith, and vision for your life. Let this be a phone call from the heavens saying, "I want you."

Your own belief in yourself is not as important as your obedience. Your confidence does not factor into the equation. God's confidence in you will overcome whatever fears, you are facing.

Right now, focus on the obedience that is required of you to move and shift forward.

Keep going ahead step-by-step, or in leaps and bounds.

You are believed in!

NOTHING IS IMPOSSIBLE FOR YOU

If nothing is impossible with God, nothing is impossible for you. Others may think that you don't have what it takes. They can see that you lack the qualifications. There might be blank sentences that need to be filled out in your life. True, so true. But advance is not just pure math and statistics. Advance is heart.

God sees who you are – deep down inside. He knows what you are capable of. So He's going to advance you. His favor and kindness are going to make people want to do special things for you. God's stamp of approval on your life will function, better, than a diploma, or a graduate degree.

And when you fail, you can ask for mercy. But no matter how many times you fall down, God's plan for you remains the same.

Mercy is what makes your enemies jealous. They did not ask for mercy, and thus are hardened in their hearts. Mercy is what God is famous for.

And because you are asking for mercy at this time, your humility is seen in heaven. Mercy reaches down and picks you up, and puts you in the right place again. Mercy is what will advance you.

Mercy from God is incredible! It does not depend on your worthiness, or even on your humility.

Everyone knows you were the last choice. Everyone knows you are the underdog. But as in the movies, the producer always ensures that the underdog will win!

SMILE: EVERYONE'S WATCHING

The apartment building where we were living had just installed some new security cameras. A small camera was hooked up to the main door, and each apartment had a tiny TV screen from which to view the apartment's comings and goings. Some people even had the security footage playing on their main television as well.

So from your apartment, you get a pretty good view of who is walking up the front entrance to the door. You would know who had visitors, and you could always watch the kids playing in the doorway. Everyone's conversations through the intercom were being broadcast. Very entertaining!

Anytime, someone would come to the door, all the apartments' TV screens would turn on. In fact, some of the housewives in the building made it a hobby to sit, and watch all the comings and goings in the building.

The neighborhood where we were living was very, very religious. When our services aired on the national news, many of my neighbors, and other people in the neighborhood ostracized us.

One evening as we arrived home, the neighbor lady came out on her balcony, and started shouting at us.

Some other kids put deep scratches on every side of our van, along with some writing. A note was stuck to the windshield, "Foreigner, go home!"

Next, neighborhood pressure built up on the landlord to have us kicked out of our apartment. Although our landlord was very apologetic, he told us that we would have to leave soon.

"Look, I really like you guys. You are nice people, and you always pay your rent on time. But I have a lot of outside pressure trying to get me to evict you," the landlord confessed.

One evening, Mary Jane called me. "Ian, don't come home jst yet. There are a few men gathered outside the apartment. They are giving out pamphlets to passersby, and protesting against us."

Even our dog could say she was having a rough time.

The little boy from the other building started using his pellet gun to shoot at Mighty our dog.

Ouch!

From then on, coming home to our apartment building was not very comfortable for us as a family. I would pull up to the apartment building, and then we'd all get out of the car.

Mary Jane and I, Joy and Josh would head up the sidewalk towards the building with the camera glaring right at us.

"Okay kids, smile!" I'd say.

And we would all put on our best smiling, forgiving, and accepting faces.

After dropping off my family, I would park the car farther away so as not to get it scratched up again.

JUST KEEP A TWINKLE IN YOUR EYE

When things are not going right, and everything seems to be against you, just smile. Joy is the measurement of commitment and consecration. That security camera has a purpose. It will keep you smiling. Cameras can be like an attitude correction device.

By nature, you are happy and lighthearted. As you look for the humor in every situation, you will remain upbeat. Keep trying to be someone who can laugh at their mistakes, and enjoys getting together with other folks who like to laugh. Cherish the lighthearted moments.

You look great with a smile on your face. Keep that smile, keep shining, and believe. The Scriptures say how you will walk with your head held high, and every yoke broken off your shoulders.

Keep that twinkle in your eye. Always laugh at jokes! Stay upbeat.

The best way to keep your head high is to smile. The byproduct of smiling is that it knocks the heaviness, and shame off your shoulders. The blame, and guilt are not part of your work clothes, they are not a part of your dress-up routine.

You might feel that shame is something you will never get away from. But that is not true.

Remember that blame, and shame are not real good motivators. They are actually the feelings that bring confusion to your life. Don't become so introspective, that you start to sew buttons on that coat of condemnation, and think it's yours.

You will come out of the muck, and mire to stand on the heights. This is who you are.

As athletes train to win, they have to be on a good diet of healthy foods. Condemnation is not a meal you are allowed to indulge in. Don't allow others to browbeat you and don't put yourself down. You are a great-hearted runner. Feeling bad is off-limits to you.

Stay on course. Stick with the diet. Your first prize medal is within your grasp. Don't let up now.

You will come out on top. The cream always rises to the top. So, if someone asks you how are you doing, just say, "I'm winning and I just got my 2nd wind."

Look in the mirror, and just say, "I'm not an average person."

Say, "I am cream, and I am rising to the top."

IT'S A HAPPY LIFE

CHAPTER 23

CELEBRATING LIFE!

Suddenly, a high-security police bus drove up, and parked right behind us. With perfect precision, 24 riot police marched out of the bus. It was impressive.

Each policeman had a helmet, held a large shield, and wore protective body armor. Their legs were covered with protective shinguards, and their bulletproof vests and clubs just added to the whole effect. These guys were certainly ready for action!

Everyone stopped what they were doing, and just stared.

Marching in perfect unison, they stood in formation directly behind my team and I. The leader of the squad stepped forward.

"Sir! We are your security."

Then, three plainclothes police detectives stepped out of an alley. The leader walked over to me, shook my hand.

"Sir! We are here on duty," he said.

HERE TO PROTECT YOU

Everywhere I moved, there was police protection on the street for my team, and I. As our team distributed the Turkish New Testaments to those who wanted one – the squad of riot police stood there - on guard, fierce and strong.

Amidst the crowds, as thousands of people passed by on this pedestrian street, anyone who wanted a Turkish New Testament could come, and safely receive it.

One of the head riot police came up to me.

"Pastor, we want some Turkish New Testaments too. Please, the men have requested a box of Turkish New Testaments."

"Of course! Your men are doing a great job!" I said.

A CANDIDATE TO LIVE THE HAPPY LIFE

Many of you have never had people who would affirm you. You might have never heard from your own father the affirming, encouraging words that you need for life.

It's time for you to have that now. It's time that someone speak over you who about you really are – deep down.

Right where the rubber meets the road is the fact is that you are special. You were born to win.

I see in you an incredible motivation, passion, and talent. You are like a diamond that sparkles when seen from different angles. And you have that sparkle because you've been cut from the rough.

You've never stopped, and continually you still find strength to keep trying. Because you're still here. You are a true overcomer. Motivation and strength is pouring out of you.

You are chosen by God to live the happy life. You have the capacity to change history, to bring comfort into the lives of the lonely.

Even if your marriage has failed, you are not labeled as a failure. If your father has not been around, or you feel like you have lost your childhood, you are still a candidate to live the happy life.

You are not designated to be deleted or drag and dropped into the trash, because of your past. You belong on the rocket launch pad, because of the potential that is written on your heart.

Even if you are shamed, and disgraced in the eyes of some, you deserve many more chances. Your bad works cannot dominate your destiny. Your failures do not dictate your future.

You may consider yourself the worst or most irresponsible… However, this just sets you up to receive from the bank of unconditional love.

You are destined to win.

SMILE AND WAVE

As Yasemin opened the mail that had come in, she was surprised to see an envelope whose return address was labeled "Haci Bektas".

She knocked on my office door. "Ian, there's an envelope here from Haci Bektas, the place you and the team got arrested, and almost got deported."

I reached for the envelope, and opened it. "Yes. That was the place. Hmmm… They are inviting us to come back again this year."

I announced to the team about the trip, and everyone began to get ready. Packing my bags to go to Haci Bektas, my mind rebelled, but my heart knew that what we were doing was right. Going back to Haci Bektas would be a risk.

Our team finally arrived in the little town, and we set up our booth. I wondered about a suitable strategy if I saw the same police who had arrested us again.

Early the next morning, we prepared for the influx of crowds who would begin to come by 10 o'clock in the morning.

But what should appear coming down the street, but a police car entourage! The cars stopped right in front of our stand. The town's Chief of Police stepped out.

I was trembling in my boots. Not again!

I'd already been arrested in this town once, no way was I going through all that again.

NO HARD FEELINGS

I found the Police Chief staring at me, studying me curiously.

"Hi. I'd like to invite you to have tea with me at my station. Are you available, let's say… at around 2 o'clock?" he said with a smile.

"Okay, 2 o'clock sounds good. We'll be there," I replied.

But of course an invitation to drink tea from a Police Chief is not optional, it is mandatory in Turkey. After the Police Chief, and his men left, I paced back and forth in the stand.

Well, this sure is quite a turn of events. I hope we are only going to drink tea there. I thought with a bit of trepidation.

Two o'clock arrived before I was ready. We drove up to the police station, parked right in front, and marched in the door.

Who should greet me, but the very police that had arrested me last time.

"Greetings! Have a seat while we inform the police chief that you and your people are here."

He turned, and knocked on the Chief's door, pulled it open a crack, and gave the message.

When the officer returned to his desk, I was wondering at the noticeable difference in his manner towards us.

"How are things with you?" the officer said sheepishly, "Well, this is quite different from the last time. I guess it is just evident that things do change in Turkey very rapidly. No hard feelings, I hope"

Within minutes, we were ushered into the Chief's office. He was very kind, and accommodating to us. Sipping my tea, I couldn't help but think about the last time I was there – as a prisoner.

CHANGE YOUR PERCEPTION

Destined to win, that is who you are. When you look in the mirror, what is actually there is an amazing amount of strength, courage, boldness, and motivation.

Your courage is coming out in every little step that you take towards your dream. Your confidence is being multiplied because of your ownership of your vision. You have the strength.

As you look in the mirror, wipe away every lie of ugly, and look carefully to see the layers of beauty. Your beauty is significant and you wear your beauty well. Because you've come to the end of yourself, your trust is in God alone now. You have both the inner and the outer artistry which is unmistakable.

You have been trained that when you look at yourself, all you see is blemish. However, the real you inside is different than your own perception of yourself.

You see someone who is struggling, I see a contender. You see mistakes, I see the underdog that wins. You see the ugly duckling, I see the swan in you.

You have what it takes!

YOU CAN OVERCOME YOUR FEARS

And last but not least, the time came for me to return to the city where I was served cake in jail.

I was understandably nervous, as we made our way through this particular city to deliver the New Testaments to a bookstore.

The last time, I had sat in jail for three days. And so now, I just wanted to deliver the books, and then get out of the city.

Now, the storeowner where I brought the books was a kind man.

"I have a surprise waiting for you. Please stay," the storeowner constrained us to sit down, and have tea.

"This man here is the religious head of our city. He has wanted to meet you."

A tall man stood up, and offered his hand.

With a smile, he said, "I've heard so much about you. Here, please sit."

"It's a pleasure to meet you too," I said as I took a seat.

That afternoon was amazing. We talked about everything, from our families to soccer.

We were both glad to have made a new friend in each other.

I never dreamed that I'd return to the city where I had been kept in jail, and this time spend an afternoon with the main religious leader of the city!

Last time, Joe and I were locked up. This time we were treated as important guests, by the government appointed religious leader of the city.

We went from being fingerprinted and treated as criminals, to the city's head of the mosques showing us true Turkish hospitality.

YOUR BIRTHDAY CARD

Each time it is one of my children's birthday, I write them a letter with my well-wishes for their next year. Here's yours.

"Dear Reader,

You are going to take charge of this next year. Your days will be full of fun and open doors. God is multiplying your talent because of your relentlessness.

Because you are giving of yourself, you don't have to lack. This is not just a time for other people - this is your time. It's your turn to slide into home plate, hit the home run, and be the MVP (Most Valuable Player) in the game called the happy life.

You are especially growing in confidence and beauty. You are becoming stronger. No one can stand against you, all the days of your life. Those who have opposed you will disappear (or invite you to drink tea).

You will achieve in your workplace.

Good things will happen to you.

You will be in the right place at the right time.

People will have a good opinion of you.

You will make good friends. Your relationships will increase and deepen.

Your mind will be keener, and your eyes will see opportunities.

Because you are a winner!

Cheers,
Ian"

DR. IAN HERINGA

AN EXCITING LIFE IS WAITING FOR YOU

Life has been full of adventures. I've been through many situations. And I know that you too are going to come out of your problems.

According to exaggerated reports, the government claims that I have distributed over eight million (8,000,000) Turkish New Testaments. It is reported that I employ over 150,000 staff. A well-publicized urban myth says that we put a $100. bill in each and every New Testament. Our budget for that is supposed to be 800 million dollars.

Turkey's Prime Minister Erdogan said to reporters, "Stop yelling at me, because they are distributing New Testaments!" after we distributed 54,000 Turkish New Testaments on the streets of Turkey's major cities for 10 days.

The Parliament issues a statement like, "How come this Canadian is free to do whatever he wants? How come nobody stops him?"

That's why I know that nobody can stop your dream!

For the past 25 years, my team and I have distributed New Testaments in every single province, and major city in Turkey. I have jumped over fences, slipped out of side doors, and hid in the most unusual of places.

But now, "…Virtually every person who has become a Christian in Turkey has done so by first reading some portion of the New Testament."

I know that you will be protected, and hidden from whatever, or whoever comes against you.

With the Turkish Secret Service sometimes attending my church – it has been quite a ride! One year, I was called into the police headquarters every single month.

We have counted at least 5 private detectives that have been on my trail. Military officers are assigned to shadow me.

With bomb threats, and assassination plots, life is never dull. In fact, I thank God for a fulfilling life.

There is an exciting life waiting for you!

As we have been through these pages together, you have realized that you are one very special person. You have been created with unlimited and extra potential.

Only God knows the combination to unlock the safe, that reveals all the valuables inside you. God is intent on bringing out all your capabilities. You are being developed, and reconstructed!

Don't be hard on yourself if you see a lot of construction mess, or debris laying around. There is in fact great progress being made in you. You have been doing really well, and it's going to get better. This is the time in your life that good things can begin to multiply over you. Every single one of your efforts, and good attempts are to be applauded.

In the center of your change, progress, and advancement is the happy life. I congratulate you and applaud you, for all your efforts, and in all that you have overcome to this point. You have done really, really well.

So be happy! Be happy with yourself. Be happy that God loves you unconditionally.

You can win in life because it is part of the design of God on your future. God is for you! You are being carried.

Live life to the full! Enjoy yourself! Congratulations, you are loved!

DR. IAN HERINGA

The End

DR. IAN HERINGA

ABOUT THE AUTHOR

Dr. Ian and Mary Jane Heringa are the founders of ASLAN International, a non-profit organization whose mission is to "build up nations by building up people", and bringing aid to the poor. Referred to by several sources as the "pioneer of New Testament distribution" in Turkey, Ian has seen over half a million (500,000) Turkish New Testaments distributed. Having been on the "WANTED" list as a Christian Pastor in Turkey, Dr. Heringa has been arrested and harassed by the police and military over 50 times. His keys to living a happy life have been learned through the many adventures of living and working in Turkey for the past 25 years. Ian holds a Doctorate of Ministry, and a diploma in Mechanical Engineering Technology. His wife Mary Jane holds a Masters Degree in Ministry, and a degree in Speech Communication and Theatre Arts. Ian and Mary Jane have two grown children, Joy and Joshua.

IT'S A HAPPY LIFE

IT'S A HAPPY LIFE

Made in the USA
Charleston, SC
28 November 2012